CAVALIER
CHRONICLES

D1350607

ISBN 978-1-909121-62-1

Acorn Independent Press

CAVALIER
CHRONICLES

With words from Rufus,
Chip, Reuben and Hugo

LJB FRASER

Extract from *The Twa Dogs* by Robert Burns

"When up they gat, an' shook their lugs,
Rejoic'd they were na *men*, but *dogs*;"

Translation;

When they got up, and shook their ears.
Rejoiced that they were not men, but dogs.

DEDICATION

To Skye, my inspiration and the future.

What you think about yourself is much more important
than what others think of you.

Contents

Foreword ix

Introduction xi

How it all began, By Mistress xiii

Chapter 1	The Special Trip 1
Chapter 2	Reuben Comes To Stay—And So Does Mum 9
Chapter 3	My Peace Is Shattered 17
Chapter 4	Our Lovely Walks 23
Chapter 5	What's This? 27
Chapter 6	The Walking Tree 31
Chapter 7	Reuben Stays For a Long Time 35
Chapter 8	Reuben Visits Rufus 39
Chapter 9	Something Strange is Happening 45
Chapter 10	It Smells Like a Dog 50
Chapter 11	What's Happening to Me? 53
Chapter 12	It's Still Here 57
Chapter 13	Silly Me 60
Chapter 14	Home From Home 64
Chapter 15	Something Mistress Calls "Ring Craft" 70
Chapter 16	Visiting Gran and the Other Ladies—
I like The Coffee Mornings Best 73
Chapter 17	A Dog in a Bag? 77

Chapter 18   I love the Vet Sometimes.. 79

Chapter 19   The Big Outside 84

Chapter 20   The Joys of Liver Cake.. 88

Chapter 21   Is Darlington Ready? 92

Chapter 22   I Love Primrose.. 98

Chapter 23   Loving and Leaving 102

Chapter 24   Goodbye Chip 106

Chapter 25   They're Not Dogs—So What Are They?...................... 109

Chapter 26   A Waggy Tail then Down in the Borders..................... 115

Chapter 27   Going to Kennels 121

Chapter 28   Is This Another Holiday?..................................... 125

Chapter 29   Just Another Cavalier Club Show 127

Chapter 30   Staying with Skye and Sarah... 130

Chapter 31   Going to Crufts 134

Chapter 32   A Very Long Drive... 138

Chapter 33   Rufus.. 141

Chapter 34   Home at Last.. 146

End Note.. 149

Foreword

When my friend LJB told me the manuscript of Rufus, his pals and their antics was finished and asked me whether I would like to read it, I embarked on the task with a degree of trepidation as over the forty odd years that I have been breeding and showing Cavalier King Charles Spaniels, I have read a lot of 'doggy' stories and have found a lot of them rather overdo the sentimental aspect of the subject.

I need not have been concerned; the amusing, sometimes sad, but always original stories of the activities of Rufus, Reuben, Hugo and their pals had me captivated from page one. The account of dog showing is particularly entertaining and I am sure it will bring a smile to the face of many a reader. It is described from a very different and original view point.

I feel this story will be a pleasure to read no matter what the age or background of the reader.

Personally, I am already looking forward to the sequel.

Ken Town

Barsac Cavaliers

INTRODUCTION

Hello,

My name is Rufus. I live a lovely life with Mistress and The One With The Beard. I have a big house and an interesting garden. We love our walks in our park, it's called Colinton Dell. I've been on at Mistress for a while to share my story, so she's agreed to translate it into human words. I've been desperate to tell everyone about the fun I have with my doggy friends. But I'm not the only one in my house. The other dogs I live with now—Reuben, my brother, Chip and the new puppy, Hugo—all want to help me tell my story. Well, you know how jealous dogs get, so I suppose I'll share the storytelling. Oh, and there's a cat called Kitty here too, and although it goes against the dog code, I've agreed to let her join in. She's not like other cats because she plays with us and grooms us. Other cats are strictly for barking at and chasing. We wouldn't dare do that to Kitty—she's got sharp claws.

Anyway, we dogs have a hobby. We take Mistress to shows where she can win prizes if she behaves well. There's lots of talk at the shows about "The Big One". I believe it's a show called Crufts. Mistress is really keen to qualify for it.

So here we go. This is my life story for the first three years. I wanted to share the fun we have, some sad times and the scrapes we get into. I've allowed Mistress to start the book, but then we all join in.

Barkingly yours,

Rufus

How it all began, By Mistress

I held him close as I sensed the end was coming. We'd been told to expect it, and knew it was his wish to die at home. The fire was warm in the lounge as he lay on his favourite couch. He loved the garden view from here. The autumn sun had faded from the window. His eyes were closed now, and as a tear escaped down my cheek, I knew his eyes would never open again. I sensed his time was up when his breathing got shallower.

I knew he'd be happy to die here in the peace of the warm familiar room with the coal fire that he loved so much. He'd been wonderful to know, and full of fun. He had been much loved by all the family, and all those who had known him. All was peacefully quiet with only the clock chimes to signal the hours we'd been here with him. Occasionally one of the children would bring through a cup of tea, shed a few tears and kiss his head or stroke his cheek.

The death of a loved one is never easy, but in a way I was pleased he was dying at home with the family around. We were all there: me and my three grown up children who had come home to be with him at the end. How they'd loved him. He was a huge part of their lives, always there when they needed him. He was old now and had always been healthy, so I knew in my heart that although this short illness was taking him away from us, it meant no more suffering for him. The gap he would leave in our lives was unimaginable. All through his life he'd given us everything—his love, loyalty and his hard work—and we loved him for that.

Then it was time for them all to gather around to say their last goodbyes as he quietly sighed and prepared to leave us. We all looked at each other, uncertain of what to do. Although he was barely conscious, we all thought he seemed to smile with his last breath. When I realised it was all over, I could feel the hot, overwhelming tears begin. We all held each other, and even at that dawn of grieving we began to share all our wonderful memories of him. Even our dog, Chip, and the cat, Kitty, seemed to know what was happening.

I gently lifted him off my lap and into his basket. Our beloved Tibetan Spaniel, Gizmo. I could never replace him. Our fourteen-year-old Longhaired Chihuahua, Chip, would be quite lost without Gizmo. Maybe we could think about a puppy in a while.

"I'll take him to the vet now. He's at peace and he'll be with all the others." I said, my grown up children all sobbing like little children, remembering our faithful dog and all the other pets we had loved and lost. My faithful German Shorthaired Pointer, Duke, many years gone now, but still much loved and missed, would look after all the wee dogs that followed him.

I think if we got another pup, it would have to be a Cavalier. Ruby coloured, of course, like the two other Cavalier King Charles Spaniels that I have owned over the years. I got Brandy when I was fourteen, and from then on was a committed fan of the breed. Then when the children were young, we got Ben, and wept when we said goodbye to him. Gizmo would join them, Duke, Brandy and Ben, in whatever doggy heaven there was.

CHAPTER 1

The Special Trip
14th November 2009

Rufus

I was exhausted. It happens every time when we come back from a special trip. Exhausted but very happy. And they're all happy too— with me, little ruby-coloured, talented me.

My name is Rufus. And I'm a dog, a very special dog—a Cavalier King Charles Spaniel. At least that's what The One With The Beard and the one who gives me lots of treats think. And also what the one in the big wheelie chair who they call Jodie thinks. The One With The Beard and the treat-giving one seem to have lots of names, so I'm not sure what I should call them. I live with those two. I'll just call them Mistress and The One With the Beard. That might make things easier for you, as you're probably a human reading this. Dogs don't need to read. We just know, well most of the time. Jodie only comes on weekends when everyone is at our home. I like to jump on her bed when she's here to wake her up. She laughs when I try to give her my very best licks. It's what they all call "A good Rufusing".

I was lying here in my basket this morning, just thinking about my day. I was so excited that I hardly slept last night. So I woke up Mistress nice and early so we could go on our special trip. She does lots of special trips with me—just her and me. The One With The

Beard came with us once, a long time ago, but he's never come again. I'm not sure why.

Anyway, I knew another trip was going to happen when she got the black box out yesterday, along with a folding thing, a chair I think. Not a chair like the ones in the house, but a special chair she only takes on trips. Then I saw the green thing that she fills with something hot and puts in the black box. That was when I really knew that another special trip was on the cards. The biggest clue of all was when I got put in the bath yesterday, after a long muddy walk, and got washed with smelly shampoo and conditioner. Then the thing that blows hot air got me nice and dry. I like that. It blows my ears and tail and paws and gets them dry really quickly.

So, at the crack of dawn, I got Mistress to give me lots of cuddles and then my breakfast. I've got her well trained. I think it's important to train the folk you live with well. It makes life a lot easier. However, sometimes they just don't seem to understand what I'm trying to get them to do. And of course, I've trained them both differently (but more about that later). We tried not to disturb my best friend, Chip. He is a small dog, much smaller than me. I was bigger than him when I first came here, when I was still a puppy with lots more growing to do. Chip is very old. They boast about him being "fourteen and a half". But he doesn't see too well, so he doesn't come with us on our walks because he gets scared. I think that it's fine that he doesn't come on walks. He's so small that every other dog must seem huge to him.

In fact, I think he likes the peace and quiet when Mistress takes me out and leaves him behind. I know I can be a bit bouncy at times, but I'm a dog, so I'm just doing my job. Kitty the cat knows we're going out, but she just stays snuggled in her cat basket.

After breakfast and a quick trip to our big garden, which I share with the other animals and is great for playing and burying things, we headed off in the car. My Mistress put my dog cage safely folded up in the back and then put me in the front seat beside her in a harness. It's not like a collar because it goes over my back and has a very short lead that clips onto the human seat belt. I think she does it to stop me from jumping all over the car. I love Mistress, but sometimes she can be a bit of a killjoy. I sat on a cushion so that I could curl up if I got tired. I tried to stay awake and look out of the window, but whenever we're in the car for a long time I get sleepy. It's great when she lets me sit beside her in the car. Much better than the dog box in the back, although I don't mind the dog box when another dog is there with me.

Sometimes another dog comes to stay that looks just like the one in the reflecty thing in Mistress's bedroom. It took me a while to understand that the dog in the reflecty thing wasn't ever coming out to play and just barked at me when I barked at it, so I just ignore it now. But the dog that looks like the reflecty one, Reuben, is a great friend. We bounce and play and go for long walks. Sometimes he comes home with us after the special trips and stays for a sleepover. That's really fun; we play and play until we're exhausted. I can cuddle up to him. Sometimes even Chip will climb into the basket in the kitchen with us for a cuddle, but only when he's sure we won't bounce on him. We know better than to do that. Chip may not have any teeth, but he can still gives a good nip. We know our place with him, he may be a lot smaller than us, but he's a lot older, and that means we have to respect him. Apparently Reuben and I are "the same breed" and "brothers" whatever that means. I know I've been his friend all my life. I have a vague memory of living with him before I got to live here with Mistress and The One With the Beard. I just think he smells like a dog. We meet every week at a "training class". I'm not sure what that is either; I just know it's a big hall where Reuben and I take our Mistresses to try to make them do whatever we like. It doesn't always work too well because we find that sitting still and coming when they wave toys at us means we get a "treat". I'm sorry, but we just find that irresistible.

I hoped that we'd see Reuben on our special trip today. The good thing about travelling in the front of the car is that I get to see lots of things out the window. When I was a puppy I wasn't big enough to see out of the window, so now it's good to be able to look out for the horses and sheep. I like horses. There are horses in the park where The One With The Beard and my Mistress take me. The horses always stop to talk to me. They're huge, really, really huge. They snort and bend their huge heads down to me so we can say hello. At first, I was very wary of the horses, but I'm OK now. I'm glad I'm not a horse. I don't think I'd like my Mistress or The One With The Beard to sit on my back. There are very big dogs at the places we go to on our special trips but no one sits on them.

Mistress stopped the car after I'd had plenty time to have a good sleep. We arrived at a place that I thought I had been to before, at least it smelt familiar. All the special trips smell different. We usually see the same humans there. They are Mistress's friends. This time I smelt the sea. I like the beach, and all those special smells and the stuff I can snuffle and dig in—sand I think it's called. And the water is funny. It moves towards me but tastes horrid. I can hardly drink it. Every time I get taken to the beach, I try to have a drink just like I do from the river down the dell, but every time the water at the beach tastes horrid. But splashing in the funny water and chasing the seagulls is fun.

Mistress got out of the car, and left me inside while she sorted out my cage and secured it onto the trolley.

"Stay, Rufus." She warned.

Well, it was all very well telling me to stay when I was so excited, but I couldn't help myself. I just wanted to get out of the car and into my cage, so that I could get her to take me into the place where the special trip was going to be. So I bounced around the car till she was ready to let me out. I knew exactly what to do. I jumped out of the car and into my dog cage, which she closed. Then she wheeled me in the cage on the trolley and we went into a big hall. There was a sign up which I can't read, being a dog, but it must have said "Dog Show" because I believe that's what Mistress calls our special trips. It means a place where we dogs get to show off our humans. We all enjoy doing that and if they're good, they might even win a prize.

She talked to me all the time that she was wheeling me in, and I looked at her as if I knew exactly what she was saying, just trying to catch the important words I've taught her so that she knows just when she should give me another treat. I like sausage best, but I knew that if Reuben was here with his Mistress then I would be in line for a tasty bit of stuff they call "Liver Cake". Reuben has taught his Mistress to make it and give it to him and the other Cavaliers he lives with. He lives with lots of them, but he's the only dog there that is the same colour as me. Most of the others are brown and white, or "Blenheim" as I've heard say. One of the dogs Reuben lives with is called Susie. I like her. She's different to the others because she's white and black with little bits of brown. She's very pretty.

Anyway, we found a space for my cage and trolley and I could smell all the other dogs. Some looked like me and others like the dogs Reuben lives with. There were lots of other breeds of dogs there, some were smaller than me and barked a lot, and there were lots of big ones like the ones I see at the training class I take Mistress to. I'm not a big fan of barking. I feel it's over-rated. It's fine if I'm playing or if there's been a cat in the garden, but Reuben's the one for barking, not me. He tells me it's because he lives with other dogs who bark, so he needs to bark so that his Mistress can do as she's told, but as I'm the only one who has to control The One With The Beard and Mistress, I don't need to bark much at all. Of course, I think Mistress would like me to bark when I want to get back in to the house when I've been in the garden, but I've trained her to keep a look out for me coming in and open the door. Why does she think I should bark when she's standing at the door anyway? It just doesn't make sense. Sometimes these humans ask the most ridiculous things.

I was nicely parked beside all the other Cavaliers, and was ready to be let out of the cage so that I could sit on top of it. I've taught Mistress to do this all by myself. Not all the other dogs have taught their people to do this, but I know if I sit nicely on the top of the cage without jumping about, I can allow her to give me a bit of sausage, or ham or cheese. I don't mind which she chooses as long as she does it. If she doesn't do it, she knows she's done wrong because I'll try to jump down. Today it was ham—excellent. I didn't see Reuben, so no Liver Cake today. Pity. I'll have to train Mistress to make some.

In a wee while the brush came out. Again. Not that I mind, it gives me a good feeling and brings such a big smile on Mistress's face, I even allowed her to give me another bit of ham.

The Dog Show means I get to show off. We like showing off, us Cavaliers. I got her to lead me into a thing they call "The Ring", and then I got her to stand very still with a smile on her face while another human they call "The Judge" walked slowly past me and all the other dogs in the ring. If Mistress does this well then she's allowed to give me another scrap of ham. Then we all walked around the ring following each other. I got her to walk close to me and keep up with me, if she does this—more ham. Sometimes she's nervous and this puts me right off, but if we get it right then I'm happy.

Then, as usual, I got put on a table where I stood still and the other human that'd been watching us, the Judge, smiled at me and looked at my teeth—goodness only knows why, but it happens every time we go on a special trip. Some humans have really funny habits. The judge felt me all over, and then it was down on the ground to walk round the ring again. But this time I got to show my Mistress off all by myself. I thought they liked her. She stood very nicely in front of the judge. Once all the other dogs had shown off their humans, we all had to get them to stand nicely so that the judge could decide which one was the best.

When it's Mistress, she gets a red rosette and I get more ham, so I hoped she'd do well today.

She did. I jumped about to let her know how clever she is. I know red is her favourite colour so I'm always pleased when she gets a red rosette. She's always pleased to get any colour, blue, green, yellow or even white, but she seems to like red best. I think it's because it matches her handbag and the boots she wears to the dog shows and sometimes on our walks. The One With The Beard gave the boots to her when I was a pup. They looked like really good toys to play with. I tried to get her to share her new toys, but she's kept the boots all to herself—probably because they're red. I used to try to play with the long, very chewable lacing things on them but even that wasn't allowed. So I just leave them alone now. We have to respect each other's toys. After all she doesn't try to chew my squeaky goose.

I was so pleased for her today that I allowed her to give me some extra ham. All my doggy chums were pleased for me too; it's good to have a Mistress win a prize. We waited a bit longer because she had to go back into the ring with all the other winning humans. She didn't get a prize in the second round, but I thought she was happy with her red rosette—the rosette for the next round had lots of colours on it—and was not nearly as red as the rosette that she won.

She chatted to the other humans while I waited in my cage and snoozed. I was hoping to take her for a walk once we left the hall; I thought she deserved it. The humans were all chatting about the shows they go to and I kept hearing the word "Crufts". I think it must be a kind of show. Judging by how often the word comes up, it seems to be a really big one that everyone wants to go to. It would be wonderful if Mistress got to go, but it seems that it's hard to qualify to get in. I'll just have to work harder with Mistress so that she gets the chance.

So, my friends, that was my busy day. I took Mistress for her walk after the dog show. I showed her how clever I was at bouncing through the funny water, and how fast I could run when I try to catch the seagulls. I haven't caught one yet, but I'll just keep trying. Mistress sat on a rock beside the funny water. I ran up to her, and she gave me a big cuddle. It didn't even matter to her that I was all wet. I love my Mistress.

When we got home after the long drive, I carried her red rosette proudly into the house to show The One With The Beard how clever she'd been. He gave me a crunchy fish treat. You'd think he'd known we'd been at the seaside.

So I've had my dinner and I've even let them play with me, and now I'm curled up in my basket in the lounge beside the cosy coal fire that we all love, waiting for Mistress and The One With The Beard to open the bedroom door so that I can get to sleep properly. They used to try to get me to stay in the kitchen, where I'm left when they dare to go out without me, but they quickly caved in when I cried at night, so now they let me sleep in their room. Training humans can be so easy at times. I do let them share the huge bed I have there because they keep me warm. Chip, the small, old dog sleeps on his special rug beside our bed. He thinks we'd all squash him, so he's happy on his rug. You'll hear all about him later. It's even better when my brother, Reuben, comes to stay 'cause he gets on the bed with me. And we even leave enough room for my humans.

CHAPTER 2

Reuben Comes To Stay—
And So Does Mum

(August 2010)

Rufus

There was a really exciting weekend when I was young, when Mistress came home with another dog who they called "our mum". We weren't sure what they meant until Phoebe, the really pretty girl dog, explained. Reuben and I definitely recognised her. We're all the same deep ruby colour, and all our humans thought we looked lovely together.

This is what happened. Reuben came to stay on the Thursday, and I suppose I thought it would be just the two of us at first. We played and played. Thankfully, once Reuben had arrived, Mistress behaved and sat nice and still in the sunroom while we got a good play. Sometimes she interrupts us, and then Reuben and I know we'll have to do some re-training with her. Her punishment when she does this is to make her share the really smelly fish treats that she makes such a fuss of liking. We both take one so that's less for her. I do wish she'd learn to let us do what we like. She likes to think she's the pack leader. For the sake of peace we usually let her behave as if she is, but we know better really.

That night, we both snuggled up on our bed, letting Mistress and The One With The Beard have just enough room to sleep so that they didn't get in our way. Sometimes we let them watch television, but if they watch it for too long and disturb us, we creep up the bed towards them till they turn it off. It usually works. It's easy to wake them. One of us just jumps off the bed and scrapes at the door. That gets them moving in case we're going to pee indoors. Of course it means we have to go outside and pee, but it's fun to see how fast they move. Although recently I've noticed that if I do it too often, I get left in the kitchen all night; and that's not nearly as comfy as my big bed, so it can backfire a bit.

Anyway, the next day, on the Friday, Reuben and I had a big walk, and when we got back to the house we got our paws, ears and tails washed in the funny soapy stuff. Then we got blow-dried, so we knew that a special trip was on the cards. True to form, Mistress got out the chair thing, the black show box and the green flask for the hot stuff she drinks at the dog shows. She gave us a big brush, and then she went out in the car. What a cheek, the night before a special trip. We stayed to look after The One With The Beard, and got him to play with us. Then we heard Mistress's car and rushed to our chair at the window. It's a great chair, we can sleep on it even when we're wet, and it's the perfect height for us to be able to look out of the window. Reuben jumps up on it with his toy whenever he hears a scary noise. I keep reminding him, sometimes these noises come from the TV or the radio, but he keeps forgetting. Reuben has lots of toys, and we share them. He needs to hold a toy when we go for a walk, or when he hears dogs on the telly or radio, or whenever the doorbell goes. I think it's like a security toy for him.

We saw Mistress getting out of the car, and what a surprise. She had another dog with her. Reuben and I rushed to the door and waited to see who it was. Reuben was so excited that he gave his toy pheasant a jolly good shake. We wanted to give Mistress her usual welcome, but the other dog was much more interesting. It was a girl dog. She gave us a lovely greeting and Mistress let us all out in the garden. Reuben and I were sure we'd met her before. What fantastic fun: two chums. Mistress and The One With The Beard seemed to be having fun too so we let them join in.

Phoebe, the girl dog, told us that she was our doggy mum. No wonder she had seemed so familiar. She told us it was lovely to see us again and spend some time with us, but she wouldn't put up with any nonsense. As far as she was concerned, this might be my house, but while she was around, she was the boss. I guess that's fair enough coming from our doggy mum.

I haven't I've told you much about Kitty. She's a cat. She was very welcoming when she met me. I was only a pup and when I tried to bounce on her, she'd let me know that was definitely NOT on. She doesn't scratch, just pats me gently with her paw. But I'm not silly; cats have claws that they can hide. And as I don't fancy getting scratched, I give her the respect she wants. Kitty is a very pretty cat. Mistress tells people she's a "Siamese", but I know she's just a cat. She licks my face with her little tongue that is quite rough, but it feels good. And she likes to snuggle up with me in front of the fire. I sometimes see cats when I'm out for a walk and get a strong urge to chase them, but for some reason, Mistress won't let me. I don't understand it, I just want to say hello like I do with Kitty. Reuben says cats are fair game, especially the ones that live next door. He's taught me to bark when we hear them through the fence, but Mistress calls us back into the house when we do that. Kitty is the first cat Reuben has been friends with.

Anyway, Phoebe, our doggy mum, isn't so sure about cats. She thinks they're definitely for chasing. We had a big play outside with her, and then Reuben and I showed her all around the house and the garden. She seemed to like my house. But she tried to chase Kitty and Kitty got cross, puffed out her fur, arched her back and hissed at Phoebe. I'd never seen anything like it. Kitty's tail was straight up in the air and three times the size it usually is. Reuben and I tried to tell Phoebe that Kitty was OK, but they didn't really make friends straight away. After the first night though, Phoebe and Kitty got used to each other, and all of us sat on the couch together and Mistress pointed a small box that flashed at us. She and The One With The Beard do this quite a lot, and then show the box to other folk—very odd behaviour.

After our dinner, on the first night with Phoebe, the brush came out. Even Phoebe got a brush so we guessed that she might be coming on our special trip. It was great fun going to bed; there was hardly any room for our humans by the time Reuben, Phoebe and I got on the bed. We could hardly get to sleep we were so excited. I hoped Mistress would take us all on the special trip; that would be wonderful.

The next day we got up very early. I bounced on Mistress to tell her to get up. She tried to get me to go back to the foot of the bed, but it wasn't going to happen. Reuben and I started to play on the bed. That got her up. We rushed around the garden before we let Mistress give us our breakfast biscuits. Phoebe was excited too. Mistress gave us a quick brush, gathered our leads and put us in a cage in the boot of her car. Thank goodness we were all going; it would have been awful to leave one of the others behind. We were too excited to lie down and sleep, so we all hoped it wouldn't take long to get there. Today the trip was short. Reuben was so excited that he held his goose for the whole journey.

When we got to the dog show car park, Mistress parked the car and got the show cage out. Then she unfolded it and put it on the trolley. When she'd clipped it on, she put us in the cage. It was a bit of a squeeze with the three of us, but I noticed she had another cage with her, folded up on the top of the cage we were in. It was a long walk for Mistress to get in to the show. It was huge and outside, rather than in a hall.

I couldn't believe how many dogs were there—they were everywhere. All shapes and sizes. Some with hat things on, curlers in, coats on—it was incredible. I heard Mistress talking to some of the other Cavalier humans and it seemed that this show was very special. I hear the word "championship" a lot, and with all these dogs around I knew that it must be an important show. Phoebe said that she'd been to lots of big shows like this, and that they are good fun. It must be because she's older than Reuben and me that she had been to these shows before, because we'd never been to anything like this.

Mistress parked us beside all the other Cavaliers and set up the second cage. Phoebe got put into that one. I think she got a bit fed up with us pups jumping all over her. But we were side by side, so we could still see and speak to her.

Mistress got herself settled, and then got me out of the cage for a brush. I realised that we were not outside anymore, but in some kind of huge tent. I could see hundreds of dogs in this tent alone— this was a massive dog show. I hoped Mistress wasn't too nervous. I imagined her winning a rosette here. I would be so proud. I tried to keep her calm and hoped that she would perform well. I thought she was a bit nervous because she talked to me lots and had already given me little bits of ham. After my brush, she put my show lead on and we went out of the tent for a bit of a wander.

I'd never taken her to a show that is all grass underfoot before. It was much better than some of the slidey floors she has to walk on at some of the other shows. I always worried that she might slip and do badly. We got back into the big tent, and I got put back into the cage beside Reuben. Then Mistress did the same brush and walk with Reuben, and then Phoebe. I must admit that we were all looking good. I thought the judge might look at us more than Mistress, and that we could help her win if we could attract the judge's attention. I wondered if she would take us all in together. That would have been fun, but Reuben and I would have found it hard not to want to play. I'm not sure if the judge would have marked Mistress down for that.

A little while later, I was taken out of the cage and given yet another quick brush. Before I had time to protest, I had to take Mistress into the ring. Well, that solved the problem: we were going to have to take her in one at a time. No wonder Mistress was a bit nervous. We did our stuff in the ring. There were a lot more Cavaliers in the ring with me than usual, so it was a lot harder for my Mistress to win. We did our final standing still, and I could feel that Mistress was quite anxious. The judge walked past. I knew that someone else was going to win. I was just about to jump up on her to let her know that she shouldn't worry—I think she's the best Mistress anyway—when she was asked to stand in the short line of humans that the judge picked out from everyone in the ring. There were just five humans in the line, all the others were asked to leave the ring. Even though she didn't get the first red rosette, she got a white one and seemed delighted. I knew that meant that there were four winners in front of her, but she had such a big smile that I knew this prize was important to her. I couldn't wait to tell Reuben and Phoebe, and so I pulled her out of the ring quickly.

I hardly had time to say anything to Reuben, because Mistress took him out of our cage and put me in. Reuben had to take her back into the ring immediately. I barked to him to let him know that Mistress was a bit nervous. I couldn't see what was going on because there were too many humans in the way. Its difficult when I can't see her to check on how she's doing, but one of Mistress's friends spoke to me, and I got an extra bit of sausage so I tried not to worry.

It felt like Mistress had been away for a very long time. Then I spotted her and Reuben. She'd got a blue rosette. Reuben was delighted. When he got back in the cage, he said she did very well. He thought I settled her down enough for her to do much better this time. Maybe by the time she went in with Phoebe she'd be first and not second.

A lady came over to see Mistress. She had white hair and a posh voice. They laughed and talked about us dogs. Mistress showed her the prizes that she'd won so far. The other lady seemed very pleased. Phoebe got very excited, and we realised that this lady is the one that Phoebe is in charge of. The other lady got Phoebe out of her cage, brushed her, and took her into the ring. What a shame it was that Mistress didn't get the chance to let Phoebe help her win another prize, but Mistress seemed happy. We couldn't see what Phoebe was doing because the lady took her to another ring where the girl dogs were showing their humans, and Mistress went too. She didn't seem to realise that we wanted to know how our mum was doing.

After what seemed like a very long time we saw Phoebe leading the lady towards us. She had a white prize. Our special trip was wonderful with both our Mistresses winning. We all sat happily in our cages while Mistress chatted to the others. Again we heard talk of Crufts. It seems that the blue rosette Mistress won means that Reuben can take her to Crufts. I'm pleased for Reuben, and hope I can go with them. Then there was more chatting as Mistress packed up her stuff. She shared the left over ham, and then wheeled the cage back to the car.

Reuben and I felt very sad when the other lady took Phoebe with her. We liked being a gang of three. We hoped we would see Phoebe again soon. I like girl dogs, and I especially like my mum dog; I think Reuben does too.

It was a good weekend, that one. Reuben got to stay for lots of sleeps, and then his Mistress came to my house and took him away. I hate it when that happens. I love my pal, Chip, but he's very small and very old and when I try to play with him he sometimes snaps at me. I know he's the boss dog, but a wee play would be nice. I don't like it when Chip snaps. He doesn't hurt me 'cos he's got no teeth, but for a very little dog he can sound quite scary. I sulk when Reuben goes home. Mistress doesn't seem to realise what good friends we are. Sometimes I even try not to eat after Reuben goes back home. If I refuse food from Mistress, maybe she'll get the message that Reuben should stay here. I suppose Reuben would miss his Mistress, but he'd get to see her at shows. I love having him here. Maybe one day Mistress will get the message.

CHAPTER 3

My Peace Is Shattered

Chip

Hello there. I am the boss of the house because Mistress and The One With The Beard have belonged to me for a very long time. I might be the smallest of all the dogs, and I may have no teeth left, but I expected a bit of respect and I generally got it. Apparently I'm a Longhaired Chihuahua and they call me Chip. A very long time ago I had another Mistress, but she stopped living here. Her name is Sarah. She still visits and gives me lots of cuddles, which is nice. She sometimes brings a very small person called Skye with her. The very small person likes to give me treats, so even though I get a bit scared when the small person bounces, I do like it when she comes to stay.

When I first came here as a pup, there was another dog here, Ben. He looked just like the Rufus dog that lives with me now. Gizmo was here too. I loved our gang of three, and was very sad when Ben died. He was old, and couldn't see, so if he wandered off when we went out for a walk, Gizmo would run up to him and guide him back to Mistress. She always thought this was very clever, but it's just that we look after our own and if one of us needs the other we're there. Mistress once moved all the furniture round in the lounge, but Ben got really confused and started walking in to things. Gizmo and I knew he'd been blind for a while, but Mistress obviously didn't realise. Why should she? She's only human. With Gizmo and me acting as his eyes, Ben coped really well. Mistress put everything back in it's usual place once she realised that Ben couldn't see, and took him to the vet, David, to confirm what we three dogs had known for ages: that Ben was blind. That's when she noticed how Gizmo helped Ben on our walks, even though he's been helping Ben for ages. Humans can be a bit dull in their senses sometimes. Just as well they've got us looking out for them.

A few years later, Gizmo, the other dog, who was older than me, got sick. We both knew he was going to die. I remembered the day he left. I sat as close to him as I could. He was on the couch beside the warm fire that we both loved to sit beside. You heard about him from Mistress at the start of our story. All the children were with Mistress, including Sarah. I could sense when Gizmo started to drift away. Dogs just know what's happening. It's all part of life. Mistress took him away to the vet and he didn't come back. Mistress was very sad and so I was. He'd been my friend for a long time—all my life—and the house seemed very lonely without him. When Gizmo went away I just slept all day and felt very sad. I didn't even feel like eating. I'd never been the only dog in this family, and I worried about how was I going to cope.

Then one day, something odd happened. A very tall (to me) metal dog pen appeared in the dining room, quite close to my favourite radiator. That worried me a bit because I liked to sleep close to the heat, but Mistress made sure there was still enough space for my bed in front of the radiator. She put a new bed inside the pen, along with toys that I hadn't seen before and a small bowl of water. I don't bother much with toys now, having no teeth, and to be honest, not much energy to play, but this was the most interesting thing to happen in the house for a very long time. Mistress and The One With The Beard seemed much happier, so something was clearly going on. I felt a bit excited myself and the sad feeling wasn't as bad as usual.

I don't think they really understand what it's like to be a very old dog. I need to sleep a lot. At least Mistress doesn't expect me to take her to the park any more. With my eyesight going a bit, I can't see other dogs until they are very close, and that scares me a lot. And I get a bit stiff in my joints, so walking around the garden and sniffing about there is as far as I really want to go these days. My days of long walks down in the dell are definitely over. Luckily, I've trained Mistress to respect my old age. I still get her to give me little treats though; training your human never stops, no matter how old a dog gets. I keep hearing Mistress tell people that I'm nearly fifteen. Stupid woman can't count; I'm nearly a hundred and five.

Anyway, Mistress went out, and when she came back I had the shock of my life. A puppy. Imagine that, a real puppy. I hadn't seen one of those since I used to go to the park. Of course he was already bigger than me, which meant he would be a lot bigger eventually. And talk about bounce, and yap and eat—oh boy could he eat— although the real advantage was that I started to get fish, chicken, boiled egg and warm milk. I decided very quickly that this noisy, bouncing pup would be my new friend. I felt much more settled with him around. I didn't like being the only dog in the house, and this was much better. I'm so old that I had really forgotten how to play, but this new pup, Rufus they called him, and I started to have a good old bark at each other every evening at the same time, just before we got our dinner. This seemed to suit Rufus, and meant he didn't pester me much during the day when I usually sleep, but Mistress and The One With The Beard kept telling us to be quiet during our evening bark swap. It took a few days before they realised that this was us talking. It amazes me how little they understand about dogs sometimes.

Having Rufus around has made me feel much better.

Mistress now gives me horrible tablets every morning, but it means I can get up the steps in the garden and have a good sniff around with Rufus. We've got a big garden with lots of interesting things to explore. There's plenty of grass for Rufus to bounce about on, and big trees and shrubs to sniff. Mistress loves her flowers, so we don't go near them, but there's lots of space to explore so we don't have to bother with the flowers.

Rufus likes to take his bone-shaped biscuits outside and bury them in the garden, although sometimes he gets in to trouble for digging holes in the flower borders. If I go near to where he's buried one, the cheeky pup growls at me. I just stand still and give him the sort of look that makes it quite clear that dogs of the calibre of a Longhaired Chihuahua would never dream of stooping so low as attempting to dig. That's just preposterous. Have you seen my paws? They're built for gentle walking, not for getting mucky digging up biscuits. Rufus leaves his biscuits for a couple of days, and then digs them up. They're all squashy and look disgusting. It must be a Cavalier thing, but Reuben doesn't bury things—his favourite game is rolling in fox poo when Mistress takes him for a walk. He smells disgusting when Mistress brings him home. He's always really happy when he's done this; I have no idea why. She keeps him on his lead, and puts him straight into the shower. He tells me he doesn't understand why; after all he's just following instinct. Frankly, if that's instinct, it's seriously over-rated. Clearly, Reuben just thinks that this is another thing that humans don't understand. Judging by the stink the fox poo makes, I'm on the side of the humans with this one.

Rufus loves it when Mistress does the garden. She's got a patch where she grows special stuff, I think she eats some of the plants—very weird habit—and we're not allowed into her patch. She has a little wooden fence round it, too high for me, and too high for my old friend Gizmo, when he was still here. But when Rufus arrived, it wasn't long before he could jump over it. He can really bounce, it's as though he has springs on his feet. Mistress had to put a wire fence around her special patch, to make it too high for Rufus. She sometimes pulls lumps of grass and what she calls "weeds" out of the patch and throws them over the fence. I just lie in the sunshine and watch, but Rufus picks them up and shakes them. The earth goes flying when he does this. One time he picked up a big tuft of grass right next to me and shook it really hard. The earth went all over me, so I gave him a good growling. Mistress laughed, but she picked me up and dusted me off. So now I'm careful where I lie, and keep an eye on Mistress while she's doing the garden.

Another thing I've tried to teach Rufus to do is to lift his leg to pee like I do, but when he tries he just falls over. Maybe it's something to do with being a puppy. I can't remember that far back. Rufus insists on squatting like a girl dog—how silly—but I'm sure if I show him enough times how it's done, he'll learn. I wish Gizmo was still here, he'd love Rufus. Rufus keeps bringing me his toys, and in some ways I'd like to play but I keep reminding him that when a dog gets very old, puppy playing is just not dignified. I sometimes have to tell him off if he gets annoying, but then we curl up together in front of the fire and he knows how glad I am that he's here. Mistress seems very happy with our new addition, but not as happy as me.

Having Rufus here has given me a new lease of life. I didn't like being the only dog in the house. I liked having other dogs to help me look after Mistress and The One With the Beard. At my age I just didn't feel up to the job by myself. So although Rufus bounces, I know he'll settle down once he grows up a bit, and being a young dog, he's well able to train our Mistress and The One With the Beard. So I share as much as I can with him, put up with his puppy carry on, and pass the responsibility of training our humans to him. I know I won't last forever; I'm getting more and more achy and tired. Rufus is a lovely companion for me. I love cuddling up to him, and he heeds my warning growl if he gets too playful for me. And he makes Mistress happy, which is good. If she's happy she's much more likely to behave well. I love it when she puts me in the bag thing to go for a walk with Rufus. Now that my eyesight is fading, I get really frightened when I go for a walk on my lead. But in the bag, I'm close to Mistress, it feels like she's cuddling me, and I can look up and see her smiling face when I'm in there. I feel safe and cosy, and I enjoy smelling the park where I loved to run as a younger dog. People stop to chat to Mistress and pat me, which is nice. She doesn't take me every time she walks Rufus, because I've trained her to notice when I'd prefer to enjoy the peace and quiet, and would rather stay and sleep while Rufus takes her for her walk.

The sad feeling about Gizmo is fading fast, and I'm happy to let Rufus know how much it means to me to have him share the training of Mistress. I tell him how very important it is to get our humans properly trained. I tell him that The One With The Beard is very easy to train, and that he gives in to everything. Mistress is different, she likes to think she's the leader of our pack, but of course Rufus and I know that that's ridiculous. But she can be stubborn to train, so she needs special handling. The trick is to let her think she knows best, then do what you want to do. Works every time. Mistress never took me to the things Rufus describes as shows where lots of other dogs show off their humans. Sounds far too much like hard work to me. But if Rufus wants to go to all the hassle of showing off Mistress, good for him. And, quite frankly, while he's off showing Mistress, I get good day's rest, conserving my energy for when he gets home. I also tell him that it's never too early to start training our humans, and that he should hold out for the good treats. At the moment he'll accept any treats, so if he ignores the boring ones like dog biscuit crumbs and holds out for sausage or ham, that is what Mistress will give him. Otherwise the only treats he'll get will be the boring dog biscuits. I love Rufus, and I'm very glad Mistress has brought him here to join our family.

Chapter 4

Our Lovely Walks

Rufus

We've been to lots of shows now, and even one where Mistress got a red prize and Reuben's Mistress got a blue prize at the same time. We were so proud of them both. I love it when we get to go to shows when and Reuben is there. Sometimes he comes home with me and stays for lots of sleeps, but I still feel sad when he leaves, even though I'm sure I'll get to see him again soon. We have such fun together. I love it when we go for walks together down in Colinton Dell, where we can run and run and keep an eye on Mistress and The One With The Beard to make sure they're going the way we want them to.

Sometimes Mistress and The One With The Beard get upset with us when we're out on a walk. I'm not always sure why, it must be because we haven't trained them properly. They even get quite cross—although they try not to show it—like when we we're away for ages chasing a deer. We can't seem to get them to understand that's just what dogs do. We see a deer, or for that matter a squirrel—or a rabbit, and that's just that: chasing. Simple. It takes a long time for even a short chase—deer are very fast. I don't know why they worry, we know exactly where we are, because we know the dell so well. We always know exactly where Mistress and The One With The Beard are when we're out walking. We can smell them. I really do think that humans clearly can't smell nearly as well as us dogs. That must be a real problem for them.

Our dell is wonderful whatever the weather. To get there, we walk down the street, around the corner, and sit before we cross the road. This is important. If we sit, Mistress will stand still and wait. We can hear cars coming long before Mistress can, so it's important that she stands and waits by the kerb, to listen for cars or anything else that's coming. It's not a very busy road, but we like Mistress to wait before she crosses, just in case. Once we're happy there's nothing coming, we take her across the road. Then we sit down once we're at the big playing field, and wait to see if she lets us off our leads properly. It goes like this. Reuben and I sit down, then we've trained Mistress to let me off first, I give her the glove that I like to carry, and then I'm away. Reuben gives her his toy, which he has carried down to the park, and then she's allowed to let him off his lead too. Then we charge across the field, and into the dell, making sure that Mistress knows the route we've chosen.

We love to carry things, we Cavaliers. Reuben, of course, takes it to extremes. I always carry a glove to the park, and, of course, Reuben chooses a toy from our toy basket and carries it every time. Reuben needs his toy so that if he meets a dog he's not sure of, he can get Mistress to give it to him. He needs the security of his toy while he speaks to the new dog. If he decides the new dog is OK, then he drops his toy for Mistress to pick up.

Reuben's funny though, he's scared of other dogs. I can't understand it, I just go up to them with a low wagging tail and they're fine, but Reuben barks at them and goes running back to Mistress. He shouldn't be scared of other dogs because he lives with so many, but they're all Cavaliers so maybe it's other breeds he's wary of. I'll have to get him to understand that other dogs are interesting to speak to. Mistress is good with him and tries to keep him calm when other dogs pass by. The longer he stays with me at my house, the better he gets. I think it's just a confidence thing. Reuben tells me he got a big fright as a puppy, and he's not sure how other dogs will react to him, so he tries to get in first with a warning bark. The trouble is, I keep telling him, is that other dogs might not see that he's scared, and think he's being angry, which could make things difficult for him. I think he tries to understand, and when he's with me I try to encourage him to be confident with other dogs. I wish he could be with me all the time, maybe he'd get over his fear of other dogs altogether. I hope he stays for a long time this time and feels less scared. It's just as well I've got Mistress so well trained with dogs. What she doesn't realise is that Reuben takes his lead from me on our walks. Reuben is addicted to his toys, but that's just Reuben. We're all different, and that's what makes us dogs really special. Just like humans, we all have our own personalities.

Have I told you the details about our park, Colinton Dell? There are lots of paths, huge trees, bushes, hills to run up and down, long grass, big logs to clamber on from fallen trees, and best of all, a river. I hear Mistress calling it "The Water of Leith". It seems a bit odd that a river has a name, like humans and dogs, but maybe that's just another funny habit our humans have. Dog life seems much simpler. I love the dell whatever the weather. It doesn't matter if it's wet, muddy or dusty-dry; we always have fun. The big, tall trees that give shade are lots of different colours. Some folk think we dogs can't see in colours, but that's silly. We're a lot smarter than our humans think.

We snuffle around, running all over the place, while Mistress sticks to the path. She needs to do this otherwise she'd probably get lost, and luckily she heeds the training we've done with her. This means that at any one time we know exactly where she is, even if she can't see us. Just the way we like it. Then there's our favourite spot at the river. You can't imagine how good it is. There's a big bit of grass, then a little slope down to it. We've trained Mistress to throw sticks for us. We chase them into the river, pick them up in the water and bring them back to Mistress. She jumps back when we shake the water out of our coats. We can play this game for a long time, so we bark and get her to throw as many more as possible. It's great fun. When I bark to get her to throw the sticks, we've trained her so well that she throws the same number of sticks for both of us; we can count, something our humans don't know. Whether it's sticks in the river, or our biscuits after our walk, believe me, we can count.

Anyway, our beloved dell can hide some surprises; the seasons change, sometimes it's glorious with the trees full and green. Then there's the time when Mistress struggles to see us even though we know where she is, when the leaves fall off the trees and cover the ground. That's really funny. We do camouflage really well when the falling leaves are the same colour as us. We bounce about in the fallen leaves, and get back to her when we need to. We love this time of year and I'm happy to share it with Reuben.

CHAPTER 5

What's This?

Rufus

I love it when Reuben comes to stay with me. I wish he could stay with me all the time. I get sad when he leaves. It's great fun when Reuben's Mistress comes to visit, it's good to see her and she gives both of us lots of cuddles. Sometimes she brings Liver Cake, or biscuits for us, which is good. What isn't good is when she visits when Reuben is here, because that usually means Reuben is going away with her. I know he'll be back eventually, but I miss him.

There was one time, when it was very cold outside, that Reuben's Mistress came to visit. She gave me lots of cuddles, and I tried to lick her. I hoped that if I gave her an extra special face hug, she'd leave Reuben. But no, she chatted to my Mistress and Mistress gave her Reuben's lead. At least she left his bed, which meant he'd be back soon. Then he had to go back home. I was very sad. When would my Mistress understand that being with Reuben was the best thing? I did my usual sulk.

And then, after a couple of days, something very odd happened in the garden. I went running out of the back door one morning and stopped in my tracks. There was no grass, just lots of cold white stuff. Mistress and The One With The Beard seemed to think it was great fun, and even started throwing ball shaped things of the stuff around.

It seemed like fun, so of course I had to join in. What games we had. Chip didn't seem to be bothered about the white stuff, and apart from going out to the garden to pee and poo, he was happy to stay indoors. He had seen it all before. He told me it was "snow". Mistress cleared some of the white stuff from the path and the grass—it was everywhere.

Well I like snow. Even though it made my paws cold and stuck to my legs it was excellent fun. And there was more in the park. And down the dell. It seemed to be everywhere. It even covered the cars.

The whole world looked like it was covered in snow. I convinced Mistress and The One With The Beard to go for a great big walk in the snow. They said we should go to the local hills called The Pentlands. It was the first time I saw the things humans call "sheep". They were big and scary. They were very much bigger than me and smelt of wet wool. They were a grubby white sort of colour. Some of them had black faces; those ones looked the scariest. They all had staring, yellow eyes and made a very strange noise—"bleating" Mistress and The One With The Beard called it. And there were lots of them so I was well outnumbered. I got put on my lead, but I've no idea why—who in their right mind would go near a sheep? Give me a deer down the dell any day.

That first walk in the snow was amazing. We got into the car, and Mistress packed a bag with what looked suspiciously like a picnic. Yum. We drove for a while, and I looked out of the window. There was snow everywhere, even on the road. We drove in the car up to a car park beside a big hill. The One With The Beard parked the car and we all got out. Mistress and The One With The Beard were all wrapped up, and I had my cosy coat on to keep my back warm. I love my coat, it wraps round my neck and there's a strap under my tummy, so it's easy to run about while wearing it. It's dark blue, which I think goes very well with my ruby coloured coat. The snow made the world seem huge. Everything was covered in snow. Not just in our garden, but on the roads, the paths and all over the houses. I wasn't sure I would like it to stay like that way forever. It was harder to get to all the good smells when everything was covered in snow. But it was very good for digging in. The snow tickled my nose and made my paws chilly, but running around kept me warm. The sun was shining and it made the snow all glittery. We walked and walked. We met lots of people who thought I was very cute. I got lots of attention and kept jumping in piles of snow and getting stuck. The One With The Beard and Mistress laughed every time I got stuck in the snow, but they lifted me out, dusted me off and let me run again. They were having a lovely time.

We stopped at a place where the sun was shining and—joy of joys—had a picnic. It was cold sitting on the snow so Mistress put her scarf on the snowy ground for me to sit on. I got some ham, a wee bit of cheese and a couple of gravy bone biscuits. They'd even packed extra biscuits for me. I love Mistress and The One With The Beard. I got offered a drink of water, which was strange because I'd eaten enough snow to stop me feeling thirsty. Then we continued on, but the snow got deeper. Mistress and The One With The Beard kept getting their legs stuck, as the snow was so deep. I was luckier; I could just run about on top of the snow. I guess having four legs helps in snowy weather. We got down the hill and the snow got stickier. It was in between my paws and it clung onto my chest and under my legs, making it uncomfortable to walk. Mistress kept clearing the snow from under me, but eventually she had to pick me up and carry me all the way back to the car.

She took her big coat off once we got back to the car and put a warm dog blanket on her knee. I was so exhausted after the fun we'd had, that I slept on her knee all the way home. The One With The Beard drove home; he put a thing on in the car that blew hot air out to keep us warm. If I lifted my head, the warm air blew onto my ears, which was lovely. I didn't even have the energy to look out of the window. It was so comforting cuddling into Mistress after the cold snow that my eyelids drooped and soon I was dreaming about running through the snow chasing rabbits, deer and seagulls with my chums. But not sheep. They were too scary to chase, even in a dream. I woke up as the car got to my house. Mistress put me down on the snowy path and I had a quick pee before we went into the house. The coal fire was still burning, keeping the house nice and warm. The One With The Beard put a big log on it, which was soon crackling away. He moved my basket near the fire and I clambered in. I was exhausted after all the running about in the snow. After a while, Mistress called me through to the kitchen. She put my dinner down, but I sat down beside my bowl, just looking at it.

I was so tired that I just couldn't even eat my dinner. I just sat, staring at it, trying to summon up the energy to eat a little. I looked sorrowfully up at Mistress. She understood and took the bowl away. Then she made some scrambled egg. Mistress hand-fed me some of the scrambled egg, one of my favourites, but I couldn't eat very much. She gave me some warm milk with a little honey in it, which made my tummy feel all cosy. That was much better. She carried me into to the cosy lounge. I hoped she wasn't expecting me to play with her as I usually did after my dinner. But no, she put the TV on and sat on the big couch, still cuddling me. I went happily back to sleep, curled up on Mistress's lap, beside the coal fire and dreamt of snow, rabbits and a fun picnic.

Chapter 6

The Walking Tree

Rufus

I love it when Skye comes to stay. She's like a mini Mistress. She calls Mistress "Nana". She can even fit into my basket and wants to cuddle me all the time. Sometimes when I'm sleeping she kisses me to wake me up so that I can play with her, but thankfully Mistress tries to get her to leave me alone when I'm sleeping. It's very tiring when Skye is here. But the bonus is that Skye knows where all the dog biscuits are, and she can reach them. I've taught her to get me one when I want one, then if I sit and she takes my paw she's allowed to give me the biscuit. She's very easy to train. She can run around the garden and house all day, and I'm happy to share my toys with her and let her play with me. She is a bit selfish though, I'm not allowed to play with her toys and I don't think that's fair. She has such chewable toys.

There was one time when it was snowing when Skye was staying for a couple of days. She had finished her evening meal in our house and I had let her put a bit of sausage in my bowl for me to guzzle, then Mistress opened the big door in the ceiling of her bedroom with a long stick, pulled the extra staircase down and climbed into the ceiling. I find this very odd behaviour because we have a big wooden staircase in the house that she's welcome to use to go upstairs. Anyway, instead of the carrying basket for Chip that she

31

usually finds at the top of the extra stairs, she brought down a huge box. This looked very interesting, especially when Skye jumped up and down and looked very happy. When Skye does this it usually means fun.

Mistress took the box into the hall and they both started taking things out of it. I tried my hardest to help, but they didn't seem to want me to, so I settled for a tasty looking lump of wood that had fallen out of the box and I disappeared into the lounge. It was simply not fair when Mistress came through and swapped the wood for one of my own toys. Then she put the lump of wood up out of my reach on the hall table with other lumps of wood that looked equally chewable. She called this collection of wood something like "The Nativity".

Back to the box. Skye held lots of lengths of shiny stuff and shook them about. Clearly this was a sign for me to catch them, which I willingly did. Imagine my dismay when I was told to "Leave it". We were not at the dog training now, and I tried to tell Mistress that, but she was having none of it. Whoever told her to use that command doesn't understand that dogs should be the bosses. Expectantly, I allowed her to give me a treat for "leaving", but she ignored me. She wasn't remembering the bargain at all. I'm supposed to leave something alone so that it gives her the chance to give me a treat. Unbelievable. I tried again to help Skye play with the shiny stuff. "Leave it" Mistress said again. So I sulked in my basket where I could keep an eye on them both, hoping they'd see how cross I was with them. If they wouldn't play with me, they wouldn't have the pleasure of my company. Mistress compounded the insult by then telling me I was a clever boy. Don't they understand sulking?

The shiny stuff got hung up around pictures on the walls, on the staircase and in the lounge. Then they hung all the card things up on the walls, even the ones I'd managed to chew. The world was going mad.

The madness continued the next day. Skye and Mistress went out in the car without taking me. That hardly ever happens. I was on the lookout for them on my chair at the lounge window when Mistress drove the car into the driveway. It had a thing that looked remarkably like a tree sticking out of the roof. What was going on? Mistress and Skye got out of the car and lifted the tree thing out of the window in the roof of the car. I love it when she opens that window in the car. I get a lovely breeze into my cage at the back. If I lift my head up the breeze makes my ears flutter. Anyway, this was definitely a tree. It looked like the tree was walking up the path. I thought trees were stuck to the ground. I'd have to be careful next time I pee against one in case it's a walking tree.

When the tree walked through the front door, I kept my distance and warned Mistress and Skye of this terrible danger by growling. They had the cheek to laugh, and then I saw that they were carrying the tree and it wasn't walking about all by itself. That was a big relief. I was a bit miffed that they'd clearly been in the park without me, and had come back with a tree. And it was in my house.

They took it into the lounge and put it into a metal thing filled with water. No wonder I got the "leave it" treatment earlier. I thought it was a fancy bowl for me to drink out of in the lounge to save me going all the way to the kitchen for a drink. Now I realised it was a bowl for the tree to drink out of. I couldn't wait to tell Reuben this; he'd hardly believe me. Walking and drinking trees, what next?

Next was even weirder. Mistress went to the big box that the shiny stuff had come out of, and got out a smaller box. It had a big string of tiny lights in it. She put the lights on the tree and Skye helped her to put very chewable balls and other things on the tree. Once again I wasn't allowed to help, I wasn't even allowed to chew the thing that fell off, even although it looked like a dog toy. Annoyingly, all the balls and things were too high up on the branches for me to reach, even when they weren't looking. I did try, but eventually got bored. If they're mad enough to want a tree in the house and hang up

33

chewable temptations, I wasn't going to give them the satisfaction of using the "leave it" treatment over and over. When they'd finished, The One With The Beard came home from work, and he seemed very pleased with the tree. Skye and Mistress were laughing and dancing around, so I joined in. The One With The Beard picked me up for a big cuddle and showed me the tree. Still out of reach though. He called me "Happy Christmas". I gave him a big lick even though I'd never been called that before, and he was very pleased.

I wondered if "Happy Christmas" was my new name, but over the next few days it was said all the time so I thought it must be some new game the humans had thought of. There were lots of new yummy smells around, and Mistress and The One With The Beard seemed to be around all the time. Skye's Mummy, Sarah, came to visit. Reuben came to stay and lots of other people too, so I got lots of little extra treats when Mistress wasn't looking.

I hope the "Happy Christmas" game goes on for a very long time.

CHAPTER 7

Reuben Stays For a Long Time

Rufus

What an excellent day I had today. We had a very long walk this morning. I love taking Mistress for her walks; it definitely does her good. And this was a big walk. We do all sorts of walks. Sometimes Mistress takes me across the playing field and behind the wall at the top of the dell. There are lots of big trees and bushes there, so there are new smells every day.

Today we walked for a while then Mistress called out to me, "Find the wall". This is another case of human madness. The wall is always right beside us when she says this, so of course she can see it. What she actually means is "find the gap in the wall". We do this a lot, but every time we come this way, she forgets where the gap in the wall is. We can't get over the wall because it's too high, but there's a gap where the stones have fallen about half way along. We can get through that gap and back to the playing field. You'd think that she'd done this walk so often, that she'd know it as well as me by now. But no, every time she expects me to lead the way because she's forgotten where the gap is. And every time I find it, she calls me a good boy. I think she needs to concentrate a bit more, and then she'd be able to find the gap without expecting to rely on me all the time. Imagine the problem she'd have if she ever came for this walk on her own. She'd never find her way home.

She settled down after the walk and played on her typey thing, which I believe is called a computer. She tap taps at it. It keeps her quiet for hours. Me, I prefer a good bone, but I suppose that's another difference between us dogs and our humans.

She went out for a while, which she does occasionally, and that was fine because it means I got a good rest and I didn't have to keep following her around the house to keep an eye on her. Sometimes, I can be having a good doze and dreaming about chasing rabbits, and just when I'm about to catch one, she get up and goes into another room. Even though I'm fairly sure she'll come back to the room she calls "study", I have to follow her and see what she's doing. Especially when she heads for the kitchen. There's always the chance that food might be involved. Mistress doesn't usually share her food with me, but just occasionally there's a bit of cheese or ham, especially if that's what she's having for lunch. And of course, with me having such soft, appealing eyes, she just has to share occasionally and I live in hope she'll share every time.

Anyway, I was dozing on the couch in the sunshine when Mistress came through, tickled me under the chin and, as she always does, she said "Won't be long". This is a really pointless thing for Mistress to say. Sometimes she's gone for a few minutes; sometimes it feels like a long time. She must think I don't understand what time is. I just close my eyes again and snuggle down. She does the same to Chip. He doesn't even lift his head, but his tail wags at her to let her know he's heard her. I'm tired after our big walk, so it doesn't matter how long she takes.

What a lovely surprise when she came back—Reuben was with her. I was refreshed by a good sleep, and I was ready to play. We played all over the house and garden while Reuben had a good sniff to check that nothing had changed since the last time he was here. He always does that when he arrives—he likes everything to be just as he left it, so it's best just to check. He said hello to Chip and Kitty. Then Mistress took us out for another big walk—it was great.

When we got back to the house, Mistress unpacked Reuben's bag. He'd got an awful lot of stuff with him so it looked like he was going to be staying for a while. That would be great. Reuben can be a bit bossy and barky at times, but he's my best friend as well as Chip, and I'd love it if we could be together always. If only Mistress and Reuben's Mistress understood, maybe Reuben would never have to go away. I don't like it when he goes, I sulk and Mistress and the One with The Beard try everything they can to get me to play and eat. Which bit don't they get? Is it so very hard for them to work out? When I sulk it's because I miss my friend—my best friend, my brother. Don't get me wrong; I love Mistress and The One With The Beard. I love playing with them, walking them and taking them to the classes and shows, but it's not the same as having Reuben there. A dog needs friends. I love Chip, but he can't really play with me, whereas Reuben is a perfect companion.

We get up to all sorts of things together. Mistress is so easy to wind up, and we dogs are experts at that. When Reuben isn't here, my favourite trick is when Mistress leaves the hall door open and I can get into her bedroom. The door shuts behind me and I get stuck, so the only thing I can do is jump on the bed, curl up and go to sleep. Sometimes I think I can hear my name being called as I doze, but I just ignore it.

I remember the time I was left with the man who was doing something to the sunroom roof. As Mistress left to go out, she told him not to let me out of the front door. She did have a point: if the front door were open, I'd probably take the chance of a walk to the park. Anyway, the man, Chris, Mistress called him, was really nice. He smelt of dogs— not any that I had ever met, but people that smell of dogs are always good news. I hung around while he worked, successfully getting in his way so that he offered me biscuits. That worked a few times and then he put me in the hall and shut the door. What a cheek. It was my house and I was just getting him nicely trained to give me biscuits. I noticed Mistress had left the other hall door open slightly, the one that led to her bedroom, so I took the chance. I jumped up against the bedroom door to open it, trotted through and settled myself on the bed. I knew the door would close behind me and that I couldn't open it, so all I could do was settle down. I could hear the man, Chris, banging and stuff, but I just ignored him and went to sleep. A wee while later, I heard him calling my name. Well, I wasn't about to bark back. He'd banished me to the hall and wasn't calling "biscuits" so he could just carry on calling. I heard him speaking to someone, I think on the box they all hold to their ears—a mobile phone, I believe. And then he left the house. I snuggled in and drifted off. Mistress would find me when she came home. Another successful bit of human training. She even leaves a bowl of water in the bedroom to save us having to go through to the kitchen during the night, so I was sorted. What fun to have a good sleep on the bed during the day.

A long time later, I heard Chris come back in and start calling my name again. This time he came straight into the bedroom, picked me up off the bed and gave me a big cuddle. Then he took me through to the kitchen and offered me a biscuit. I had no idea why he was behaving so strangely. But I wagged my tail happily, and accepted the biscuit with due grace. He let me into the back garden and carried on with his work. This time, once I'd come back in from the garden, I just lay on the couch and watched him while I dozed. It was later, when Mistress came home and I heard them talking that I realised the Chris man thought I had escaped out of the front door and gone off to the park. And because I didn't bark when he called for me around the house, he'd gone off to the park with my lead and walked round and round calling for me, and asking all the folk out walking their dogs if they'd seen me. Then he'd called Mistress to tell her he'd lost me. She told him to go back to the house and look in her bedroom. So that's what all the cuddles were for. Humans can be very silly sometimes. I looked forward to telling Reuben about the fun. Not so sure Mistress and the man, Chris, thought it was much fun though.

CHAPTER 8

Reuben Visits Rufus

Reuben

Hello there, I'm Reuben. Apparently I'm Rufus's "brother", at least that's what my Mistress and Rufus's Mistress call me. I'm pretty sure I know what that is. I've known Rufus all my life and that we're best friends. It was a big surprise when Rufus's Mistress visited my Mistress today. I jumped higher than all the other dogs to get the attention of Rufus's Mistress. She stayed for something my Mistress calls "a cup of tea". I managed to get in front of all the other dogs and jump onto her knee. I sat there while she chatted to my Mistress. All my other dog friends tried to get up onto her knee too, but I stayed where I was. I know she likes all the other dogs I live with, but I'm sure I'm her favourite. It was a bit disappointing that Rufus wasn't with her, but great to see her all the same. I turned on my back and she tickled my tummy. I love that; my own Mistress is also very good at rubbing my tummy. Rufus's Mistress chatted to my Mistress for a while and then the most brilliant thing happened. My Mistress gave her a big bag of food, some fishy treats in a box and MY LEAD.

I was obviously going to see Rufus—I knew all the signs—and it looked like I was going on a big visit this time. I'd been before, not long ago and got Rufus's Mistress to keep me for a few days. Then I came home to my friends here, but not long after that my friend Daisy started smelling very fine and made me feel quite odd every time I was near her. Girl dogs often do this. My Mistress puts them in another room, very annoying for me, Darcy my dad, and Angus.

This time my Mistress had separated the boy and girl dogs and here was I going on a big visit to Rufus's. That was probably better for me, because as well as getting funny feelings when the girls smell good, I think my Mistress was worried that us boy dogs might get grumpy with each other. And if I went to Rufus's house, I'd forget about the interesting smells the girl dogs had, and I could just concentrate on staying with Rufus. It's great there because it's just Rufus, and me and we get all the attention from Rufus's Mistress and The One With The Beard. There's Chip too, but he doesn't really play. We give him big respect because he's a much older dog. And of course Rufus has a cat, Kitty. I like to chase cats, or would if I ever got the chance. Kitty seems different close up, and I even like to cuddle up with her, so I'm pretty sure she's my friend. I'd never chase Kitty, but if other cats stray into the garden, I'd chase them. I like to keep Rufus's garden free from wood pigeons too. His Mistress puts seeds out for the smaller birds, and the wood pigeons come down and try to pinch it. But not on my watch. I just know I'll catch one, one day, so I'll keep practicing.

Rufus lives near to a big wood with a great river for us to splash in, and I love it when his Mistress throws sticks in for us to fish out. I don't go as far into the river as Rufus does, he'll even swim in the river to catch a stick. When we're out for a walk, Rufus always leads the way. Outside, he's the boss, but when we're at his house, he always lets me get things first. Usually Rufus lets me get all the toys his Mistress plays with and throws for us, but the river sticks are different. If Rufus gets to a stick first, he won't let me have it once he's back on the bank. I do love being with Rufus, although I do miss my own Mistress. And I miss her friend, Sarah, who sometimes I have to show. She does quite well when I show her. She's a bit strict because she likes to think she knows best, but, as all dogs know, we are definitely the bosses. In fact, we are in charge. Always.

I've got lots of friends at my house where I live when I'm not with Rufus. As well as my Mistress there's Polly, Susie, Darcy, Belle, Angus, Evie, Daisy and the very new one, Teasle. I miss them very much when I'm at Rufus', but I have different fun at his house. It's great having two places where I'm loved.

I get a bit scared of other dogs, and bark a lot when I see them. Rufus's Mistress doesn't seem to understand that I'm protecting her and Rufus from other dogs in the same way that I protect my pack at home. I have to bark, to let everyone know that this is my pack, and that I am responsible for them. It's my job. It's what caring dogs do. Rufus's Mistress tries to get me to calm down. She should know better—I know what I'm doing.

Mind you, when I think about it, Rufus doesn't seem to bother barking when we meet other dogs. He just trots up to them, calm as you like, tail wagging, says hello and strolls off. I did begin to try that last time I stayed, and eventually it seemed to work. That's what I like about being with Rufus—when we're out on a walk, he's just so calm. I need to be more like him. I hope I can learn from him, and get better around other dogs. His Mistress is very kind. I think she understands. She gives me my toy when I feel nervous, and I let her give me a treat if I cope with other dogs. It's the only time I think she might be in charge. Rufus tells me that we dogs are always in charge. But as far as the walks and meeting other dogs is concerned, I do think his Mistress has a point. She knows what she's doing, and when I'm out with her, I do feel a bit better. But then it's usually just Rufus and me, so I don't have a whole pack to look after. In fact, it's only me I have to worry about, as Rufus is fine around other dogs. I do love the way Rufus's Mistress is with me. She seems to understand how I feel. I suspect Rufus has explained it all to her. I do love my brother.

But once I get back to my other home I have the pack to protect, so I do it in the only way I know, and bark to tell the other dogs to back off. When I'm with Rufus, I feel a bit safer, so maybe I'll try being more like Rufus. It's worthwhile giving it a go because I've noticed that if I ease up on the barking, Rufus's Mistress gives me a treat from the little box of goodies she carries in her pocket. I wonder if she'll still feel protected by me if I stop warning the other dogs off? It might be a risk worth taking.

I almost forgot to say goodbye to my own Mistress, I was so excited to be going to see Rufus. And I was also so excited that I could hardly choose which toy to take with me. I picked up several but found it so hard to decide. I love my toys. That's another thing that's brilliant about Rufus. No matter which toy we play with, even when his Mistress throws it, he always lets me get it first. Even if he's reached it before me, he leaves it for me to pick up because he knows I'm so mad about toys. All apart from throwing sticks in the river when we're down in the dell. Then he's in charge.

When it came time to go to Rufus's house, I finally decided on the yellow cloth doughnut. I shook it and shook it, then my lead went on and, YES—we went off to Rufus's car. I nearly wagged my tail off, it was so exciting. I jumped into the front seat and Rufus's Mistress had quite a struggle to get the dog harness on me. I tried to stop wriggling. I knew that the quicker I got the harness on, the quicker I'd get to see Rufus, but I just couldn't sit still.

Eventually we were off. I kept holding my toy in my mouth, because if I dropped it I would want to bark and bark with excitement, and I thought that might annoy Rufus's Mistress. There was no dozing in the car for me; I knew that the drive to Rufus's house wasn't that long. I looked out of the window with the cloth doughnut firmly in place. I checked out all the places we passed, and it was looking hopeful that we were going to Rufus's house. I began to recognise the roads that led there. Brilliant, I couldn't wait to see him. I gripped my toy harder when we pulled into the driveway, and then I just couldn't help myself. I dropped the toy, and instead of barking a sort of howling sound came out. I was almost as surprised at the howly sound as Rufus's Mistress. I have never made noise like that in my whole life. She started laughing and told me I'd see Rufus soon. I could see Rufus at the window standing on our chair. I know I don't live at Rufus's all the time, but I think of the chair at the window as ours because that's where we jump up to when anyone comes to the door, the bell rings or the cat next door strolls by. When that happens, even Rufus barks his head off, which is really quite unlike him. I'm not sure why we bark at the cat next door, because we live with Kitty. She's lovely and washes out faces with her tongue, which we like. I think it reminds us of being little puppies, but we don't annoy her too much because we both know she has sharp claws. You should see her climb a tree.

I ran straight to the house door once Rufus's Mistress let me out of the car. She opened the door, and I rushed in and jumped all over Rufus. He was just as pleased to see me, as I was to see him. Then we rushed around the house because I like to check that everything is as it should be. I like my routines, and I like everything to be in order. Then it's the same in the garden. I lifted my leg in as many places as possible; it's a thing we dogs do—mark our territory. I needed to mark all the places that Rufus and Chip have marked, and then Rufus followed me and marked the same spots. Then I went back to mark those spots again. Then we got a bit bored with that, and rushed about the garden again. Then it was back into the house, and of course The One With the Beard was ready to be jumped on. Mistress doesn't really let us jump up on her, but The One With the Beard loves it.

After lots of playing, and having our dinner, then getting a big run around the garden, and then enjoying a big cuddle from Mistress, we eventually settled in front of the fire. It was cold outside so Rufus's Mistress lit a big fire in the lounge for us. Although it's our fire, I expected that Rufus and I would share it with Mistress and The One With the Beard later. The coal and logs crackled, and after our big run around, we were both tired. Chip trotted through to join us, tail wagging; we all cuddled together, all happy snuggling up. The heat from the fire made us all sleepy. I drifted off to great dreams of running around the dell with my wonderful friend and brother, Rufus. I am a very lucky dog.

I do love it here.

CHAPTER 9

Something Strange is Happening

Rufus

It's been a funny week. Reuben is still here, and I'm hoping he'll be here forever. I love having him here for walks and playing. He's good at sharing my toys, and he's getting better and better at training Mistress and The One With The Beard. Chip and Kitty love him too, I think we make a good animal family. Just perfect. I think one of the good things about Reuben and me, is that as he's exactly the same age as me; we just do everything so well together. We don't even argue about food. Mistress always gives us our own special bowls for our dinner, so we know which is which and don't try to pinch each other's food. Reuben eats his dinner quickly, while I take my time. If Reuben wants more, he's trained my Mistress to give him a few more bits of dog kibble. If I leave some of my dinner, he doesn't touch it, even if he wants more. I often eat half my dinner, then come back later for the rest. Reuben knows that, and so does Mistress, so there's no problem. Chip takes his time too, and there is no danger we'd ever try to pinch his food. We'd both like to try Kitty's dinner—it smells good. Mistress puts her bowl up on a stool so we can't reach it. She can be such a killjoy sometimes.

A couple of days ago something strange started to happen. Mistress took us out to a huge pet shop that we are allowed to go in to with her. Usually, if Mistress has me with her when she goes out to the shops, I get tied up outside; I'm not allowed in. She doesn't come to this shop very often with us, but we love it because we are allowed in. This shop is full of yummy smells. We sometimes meet other dogs there, so Reuben always takes his toy.

She bought a much bigger basket for us, one that we can both sleep in properly. The one I have is fine for me and Chip because he's so small, but it's a bit of a squeeze for Reuben and me. She got us some new bedding and some biscuits. By gazing lovingly at her, I also got her to buy us a new toy. It's a pale blue toy horse thing with a squeak in it. Reuben really likes it, and yesterday he carried it to the park for our walk.

Mostly Mistress buys our stuff from another smaller shop in a place she calls Morningside. When we get in the car to go to Morningside, I'm always excited, because as well as the lovely vet, David, who lives there, my friend Alfie's Mistress has a shop there, which I can go into. It's a great shop, much smaller than the big one; it even has rabbits in cages in it. Alfie has his basket in the window so he can check out all the folk that go into his shop.

My Mistress gets the yummiest treats there, as well as our biscuits, "black pudding sticks" she calls them. They're Reuben's favourite treat in the whole wide world. He's even trained Mistress to take them to the dog shows. He's been ever so crafty. He completely ignored every other treat Mistress took to the shows when he was showing her, as he did sometimes. This made her nervous. Then one day Mistress took bit of the black pudding stick into the show ring to show to Reuben and help keep her calm. That, Reuben decided, was his treat of choice. It meant he could gaze at my Mistress, and as she behaved well, so she began to get better prizes. So now, when Reuben is in the ring with my Mistress, she gives him bits of black pudding stick. Well done Reuben, I wish I'd thought of that. I have such a clever brother.

Mistress used to take me for long walks with my friend, Alfie. It was when Reuben wasn't staying. Chip didn't come; I think Alfie would have been too scary for him. Alfie doesn't look like any other dog I've ever seen, but he's the same age as me, and I've known him since I was a pup.

Because Alfie had his bed right beside the window, he knew when I was bringing Mistress in. Alfie loved my Mistress. He always gave her a big welcome. He even jumped right into her arms, despite being twice the size of me. I don't know how he can jump so high; it must be his long legs that give him the advantage.

Mistress would sometimes put me in the car and we'd go for the very short trip to Alfie's shop. He'd allow Mistress to put him on his lead and get him into my car. Alfie didn't sit in the back with me; he always sat on the back seat. I think that's because there wouldn't have been enough room for him in the back. Mistress probably thought Alfie might squash me, but I'm sure he wouldn't. Then we'd drive for a couple of minutes, and we'd go to a very special walk place. Mistress would get us both out of the car, and although we were really excited about our walk, we'd do our best to keep Mistress calm. If she walked nicely for us, we'd get her to give us a treat because she was behaving so well.

Alfie and I loved this walk. Mistress and Alfie's Mistress called it "The Hermitage of Braid". There was a river, hundreds of trees, far too many to pee against—but we tried—and so many smells; we had fun walking there. Alfie was funny. He'd stick quite close to my Mistress, while I was happy to run ahead and check out all the wonderful smells. When we got to the bend in the river, he'd jump in and splash around with me. Mistress would throw sticks for us, I would bark—even though I don't do it often—and we'd jump around in the water having fun. I love Alfie. At the deeper part of the river, I would have to swim to catch the sticks that Mistress would throw, but Alfie has such long legs, he never had to swim. We'd meet lots of dogs, and Alfie and I would speak to them all. We'd run around and

Mistress would be so well behaved with us both, we'd let her give us a treat from time to time.

I should probably tell you more about Alfie. He is much taller than me and doesn't have a long coat like me. His coat is a similar colour to mine, but it has white flecks through it, and he has a much longer nose. He told me that he doesn't need much brushing. That must be difficult for him because I needed to get Mistress to brush me as part of the training I did with her. If she was good about brushing my coat, I'd stand still and let her practice her brushing, which was good for calming her down when I showed her. Alfie had a short coat, so I'd no idea how he trained his Mistress for brushing. When I spoke to him, he told me he didn't show his Mistress. Alfie takes his Mistress to a place where he has to run over things, through tunnels and weave around sticks in the ground. Apparently if she gives him the correct directions, and runs around a lot, she's able to give him a treat. It sounds fun, but not like the shows I take Mistress to. I keep telling him he's missing out, my Mistress loves being shown. She's a Mistress with a hobby.

When we got back from the big pet shop, Mistress put our new bed out in place of the old one. She washed the old bed and even washed the old bedding. I hate it when she washes the bedding, it takes ages to get it smelling the way it should, and then just when it smells really good—she goes and washes it again. So now we had a lovely new basket with more than enough room for Chip, Reuben and me. Sometimes Kitty curls up beside us too, so the new big bed is a great idea. Mistress put the fresh bedding in, so we jumped in and gave it a good old rumple. Mistress laughed and shook her head. She straightened the bedding, so of course we just rumpled it again. She gave up.

Anyway, then she brought in a big wire pen from the shed outside and put it into the dining room beside my dog cage. I sort of recognised it, it brought back memories of when I was a puppy, but I haven't seen it for a long time. She put it up, and placed newspaper, my old dog bed and my old bedding into it. When Reuben and I tried to get through the gate of the pen to investigate she shooed us out. What a cheek, it's my bed in there. Then, even more confusingly, she put a small bowl of water and an empty bowl in the pen. I wondered if she was going a bit mad or having some sort of delusion about having a pretend dog. I thought she was quite happy with Reuben and me without wanting to make another one up. I knew we'd just have to wait and see, but it was all a bit worrying. We had a feeling that something was going on; we dogs just know these things. Humans can easily give away what they're thinking, just by what they do. Dogs are very good at reading body language; we do it all the time. Maybe if our humans took notice of our body language, they'd be able to communicate better with us. I think Mistress is quite good at it, but that's because we trained her so well. That evening Reuben and I kept a close eye on Mistress and The One With The Beard, because they were definitely up to something. Whenever they moved around the house, we both followed. The next day, although The One With The Beard went out, we kept tabs on Mistress.

She played with the computer for most of the day, so Reuben and I could relax a little, but every time she moved we took it in turns to follow her. At one point she went out in the car, and we watched through the window till she came back. She definitely had dog food with her, but it didn't smell like our food. Later on, after The One With The Beard came home, Mistress went out again in the car and she didn't take us with her. But she did take one of my dog blankets with her. What were they up to?

Chapter 10

It Smells Like a Dog

Rufus

On the day that Hugo arrived as a pup, at first we didn't know what was going to happen. Mistress had been way for ages and ages one evening. We'd hardly been able to concentrate when we played with The One With The Beard. He gave us our dinner, but we didn't finish it. Our instinct told us that something was going to happen. The One With The Beard left the curtains open in the front lounge, which overlooks the driveway, so that we could watch for Mistress from our chair in the bay window. We kept looking, and then eventually we saw her car pull into the drive. We watched as she got out of the car. She was carrying something. She had one of our dog blankets with her, and we could just about make out something else—something that seemed to be wrapped in the blanket. She came up the drive to the front door. Yes, she was definitely carrying something in her arms. It didn't look like shopping. We rushed to the door. She shooed us away when we tried to jump up to investigate. She came into the front lounge and sat down carefully. She opened up the blanket and we saw a small animal. It looked like a very small dog. We had a bit of a sniff and, yes, it smelt a bit like a dog too. It was the same colour as us. It squeaked and both Reuben and myself sat down with surprise. Then Reuben began to wag his tail and went to speak to the little dog. Reuben seemed to really like the little dog, but I really wasn't sure.

Reuben came back to lick my nose the way he does when he's trying to tell me something. I suddenly got it. He was telling me that this was a puppy. I was astonished: is that what we looked like as puppies? A dog forgets you know. I had forgotten that once I was too small to jump up on the couch, just like this puppy.

Mistress put the puppy on the floor; his name was Hugo she told us. Hugo seemed quite bewildered. Reuben was very gentle, he seemed to know what to do—I hadn't a clue. Then I remembered that Reuben had puppies at his house. I thought I'd retreat under the table and just watch. Reuben nudged the pup very carefully, and wagged his tail. Hugo wagged his tiny tail and stood up. He was very small. He started to explore. He came over to see me, but I warned him off with a very low growl. Mistress told me not to be silly and to come out from under the table to say hello. Reuben was telling me much the same, but I was staying put, right under the table, until I felt safe. Hugo trotted round the room, having a look at his surroundings. Reuben kept close to the pup called Hugo to reassure him. Reuben was completely ignoring me. I was not feeling at all happy.

Mistress and The One With The Beard seemed entranced with Hugo, and very pleased Reuben was making friends with him. They tried to coax me out to join in, but I was having none of it. I was happy staying where I was until this pup thing went away and I could settle down with Reuben and the humans for the night. Mistress let Hugo out into the back garden. Reuben still stayed close to him. The pup had a bit of a sniff, and squatted to have a pee. Mistress was ecstatic. It was only a pee, I thought, we all do that. I went out reluctantly, had a pee and came straight back in to my spot under the table in the lounge. Mistress had ignored the fact that I'd had a pee. No praise for me, but lots for the pup. I wished it was time for Mistress to take this intruder back to where he had come from.

But Hugo didn't go home. In fact he came to bed with us. He'd even been playing with Reuben, and Reuben had enjoyed it. I felt betrayed. Reuben was my friend. And even though Mistress and The

One With The Beard tried to make a fuss of me, it didn't help. I didn't want anything to do with the pup, I just wanted my friend back all to myself. I reluctantly followed them all to bed, but slept at the bottom of the bed as far away as I possibly could from Hugo. Maybe he'd go away in the morning. Reuben did try to reassure me that puppies could be great fun, but I wasn't convinced. I was cross with Reuben too. If he'd ignored Hugo maybe Mistress and The One With The Beard would realise this pup had no place here with Reuben and me, and take it back to wherever it had come from. My lovely life was seriously at risk.

CHAPTER 11

What's Happening to Me?

Hugo

Hello, I'm Hugo. At least that's what they call to me now so I think that's my name. The Master I lived with when I was first born called me something else, but I guess I'm called Hugo now. Anyway, it suits me because when I go to the one Rufus and Reuben call Mistress or The One With The Beard, I get lots of cuddles. It's all very strange. In fact it's been very strange for a few days now, let me tell you. All sorts of peculiar things have been happening to me and I don't think I understand it all yet.

It's been a funny week. Just when I thought my world revolved around my mum, my sisters, and the other dogs, my Master took us all on a really long trip in the car. When I've been in it before, it wasn't for long and we visited a lovely man who gave me a horrid injection. But then I got a special biscuit and it didn't nip much. But this time we were in the car forever. At least that's what I thought. I really did. I thought we were all going to live in the car forever. Then eventually the car stopped. Then, joy of joys, more dogs and a Lovely Lady greeted us. She had a nice house with a garden so it was great fun. My Master gave us all a big cuddle and our dinner. I love eating, I can do it all day, at least whenever I'm awake. Then I got to have a big run around with my sisters then we all snuggled up. My sisters and I thought that we'd be there forever when another funny thing happened. Two ladies we hadn't met before came to visit. We were all really sleepy because we'd had our dinner. They cuddled us all and chatted to Master and the Lovely Lady. They both smelt of other dogs. I've already met lots of other dogs, so I knew we were safe with the ladies. If humans smell of dogs, then the chances are they aren't a threat to us. My Mum taught me that. My Mum's getting a bit sick of my sisters and me. She used to cuddle us all the time, but that's stopped now. We used to get all our food from her, but she doesn't like us trying to suckle her for milk any more. I don't really mind, because Master gives us all sorts of yummy food. I like the warm milk, the scrambled egg and the chicken with rice best. We get some little biscuits now for our dinner, like a smaller version of the food the big dogs get. I think my Mum prefers the older dogs. Apparently that's how dogs behave. She taught me that too. She taught me lots for things. But I don't seem to want her as much as I did before. So that's OK.

Anyway, after a while, one of the ladies picked me up and said goodbye to Master and the Lovely Lady. What was happening? She cuddled me in a soft blanket, took me to a car, sat in the car with me still cuddled in the blanket, put her seatbelt thing on, like my Master does, settled me on her knee, and the other lady drove us away. Hang on a minute, I thought, where is she taking me? Doesn't she know I've got sisters and other dogs I live with? I tried to tell her with little squeaky noises, but she just cuddled me in the blanket on a comfy cushion on her knee and stroked me. She smelt good, and her voice felt quite soothing. I meant to stay awake, to find out exactly what was happening, but I must have dropped off. I woke up when the car stopped. Then my lady put me in yet another car. She put something around my body and fastened it to the belt I've seen humans putting over themselves when they get into a car, just like my Master does. She waved to the other lady and started the car. I was still on the cosy cushion so I just tried to stay awake. It didn't work. We weren't in the car for very long when I fell asleep. Again, I woke when the car stopped. The lady was speaking to me softly. I liked her voice; it made me feel safe. She unclipped the belt, and lifted me off the cushion, wrapped the soft blanket round me and cuddled me close.

The lady carried me into a big house, it smelt different but there was a slightly familiar smell too. I was pretty sure I'd never been here before. She carried me through the front door and into a big room. Then she sat down on a couch with me on her knee. There was a cosy fire burning in the fireplace. I'd never seen an inside fire before like that one, and hoped it wouldn't be dangerous. A big dog, the same size as my mum came over and said hello. He was very gentle and licked my nose. The big dog wagged his tail at me, so I knew he was being very friendly. I liked him. He was called Reuben. Reuben welcomed me as soon as I got to this new home. He really looked out for me, and explained what was what. Reuben told me that the lady was called Mistress and the other human was called The One With The Beard. He told me, while we were playing, that I'd be living with them all the time and also with the other dog, Rufus. Rufus had sort of said hello but seemed to prefer to stay under the table. He didn't seem all that friendly but Reuben explained that he wasn't used to puppies. He said to give him time and he'd be fine. I am so glad that Reuben understands about puppies. It makes me feel much better.

So that's what I was then, a puppy. I'd heard folk talking about puppies in that other house, but wasn't sure what they meant. So I was a puppy and Rufus and Reuben were big dogs.

I missed my sisters and my mum but when the lady I have to call Mistress gave me some supper, petted me when I did a pee outside then cuddled me beside her on the bed, life didn't see too bad.

Now I have two new friends, Rufus and Reuben. They're much bigger than me, but they play a lot, which is good. It's a bit funny with only three of us. Well it's four really but the other dog, although it's the same size as me, is very old. His name is Chip, he doesn't play and if I get too close, he grumps at me. For some strange reason he doesn't like it when I pull on his ears or chase his tail. I thought all dogs liked that game.

I have three sisters; I miss them because they were the same size as me and we all cuddled up together. When I play with Rufus and Reuben for a while they jump up on the couch. I can't do that yet. I'm not sure if I'll grow as big as them, but instinct tells me that we're somehow all the same kind of dog, so I'm going to keep hoping. I'm the same colour as Rufus and Reuben, well nearly. They're darker than me and have lovely long ears and lots of hair on their tails. That makes it fun for me to try to catch their tails and chew their ears. I know if I'm biting too hard, because they give a low warning growl. Then I know I have to stop. They've got lots of toys, and I get to share them, which is brilliant. I'm kind of little but they've been nice to me so far—as long as I don't pinch their food, or pick up their biscuits, or bite their ears too hard. It's so difficult to stop biting. I just want to bite everything. Luckily Rufus and Reuben have lots of time for me. Whenever I'm awake, one or other of them will play with me. I love to race around the back garden, and we take turns in chasing one another. I like that game. Even though I'm much smaller than them, I can move quicker than they expect. And I like pinching a toy and trying to run away with it. But because Reuben is stronger than me, if I pinch a toy he wants, it's very easy for him to get it back. Anyway, if they don't want to share something they take it on to the couch, out of my reach. It's such a pain to be small.

CHAPTER 12

It's Still Here

Rufus

I'd been tempted to join in when Reuben and Hugo played because it looked like fun. In fact it was getting harder to resist joining in, especially when Mistress seemed to want me to. It's just that I didn't really know how, I'm so used to Reuben, he's the same size as me and Hugo seemed so small. I was a bit scared I might be too rough with him and hurt him. I might not have liked him being there, but I would never hurt a puppy. Reuben was having good fun with Hugo. He tried to bite Reuben's tail and ears, I was sure it must have hurt, but Reuben didn't seem to mind. They were having a great time playing, but I didn't know what to do so I just followed Mistress and The One With The Beard. They gave me lots of attention, which was reassuring, I just wished they'd take Hugo away, but I had a feeling he was here to stay. The metal pen thing seemed to be Hugo's place with MY bed in it. Reuben and I weren't even allowed in there. Hugo had his meals in there, which smelt great, but he didn't share any with us.

The next day arrived and Hugo was still there. I spoke to him a few times, and even sat down beside him, but Reuben seemed to know exactly what to do with him. I jumped out of the way if Hugo tried to jump on me or catch my ears. At least I could get away from him if I jumped on the couch. He's too small to get up, thank goodness. I spent a lot of time sitting on the couch just watching Hugo and

Reuben playing. I liked it when Hugo went to sleep, because then I could get to play with Reuben.

Later on that day, Reuben's Mistress came to the house. She seemed to really like Hugo. Why did everyone like Hugo except me? Reuben and I played in the garden—Hugo was asleep, again. Hugo sleeps a lot, and eats a lot. Reuben's Mistress called Reuben to her and put on his lead. This was bad news. Why did the humans keep interfering? Reuben was led away to his Mistress's car. He kept turning to give me reassuring looks. I don't think he wanted to go, because he was getting on so well with Hugo. I watched from the chair by the window and barked; trying to make them all realise that it should have been Hugo that was going away not Reuben. Reuben did try to tell me that Hugo was fun, and that I would soon be playing with him. I didn't think that would ever happen.

I couldn't even take The One With The Beard for a walk because he'd gone out. So it was just Mistress, Hugo, Chip and me. Hugo woke up, and Mistress took him outside. He didn't always make it outside for a pee. Mistress would be upset if I peed inside the house. I had thought that if I did then maybe she'd pay me more attention, but when Hugo did it she just popped him outside and cleaned it up without a fuss, so there was no point in that. When Hugo came back in, he trotted up to me and licked my nose. I knew he was trying to make friends, but I just wanted Reuben back. So I ignored Hugo, and jumped on the couch to begin my customary post-Reuben sulk. Mistress sat down beside me, and stroked me. She was trying to tell me not to worry, that I'd see Reuben soon. I just wanted him back. Now. He knew how to play with Hugo properly, I didn't.

Mistress was playing with Hugo, and clearly wanted me to join in. All this sulking on the couch wasn't making Hugo go away so I supposed I could give it a try. They were playing my favourite game. Mistress knelt on the floor and got Hugo to chase the Mr Rope toy round and round her. Oh well, I could give it a go. I jumped down, and reluctantly joined in. Hugo was very pleased to have me join in, as was Mistress. Hugo gave little puppy yaps to show his pleasure, and Mistress smiled as she played with us. He might be small, but he sure could play. He wasn't as fragile as I'd thought. It took some skill to avoid those sharp teeth though. And he was very quick. Then just as suddenly as he was rushing around playing, he lay down on the carpet and went to sleep. Mistress lifted him up gently, and popped him into the dog basket near the fire. Then I got her all to myself to play with. Maybe with Reuben gone I could get to like this newcomer. And maybe he'll get to like me too.

CHAPTER 13

Silly Me

Rufus

How could I ever have not liked Hugo? He's been here for ages and we have had lots of fun. Reuben was quite right; puppies are easy to play with. We can play tug-of-war with my toys, or the game where Hugo rushes off with a toy so that I have to catch him. Not as easy as it sounds. I tried to hide toys, but Hugo usually finds them. We turned this into our own special game. The only place I could be sure of hiding a toy so that he couldn't find it, was under a cushion on the couch. He couldn't jump up on the couch. Mistress had even bought us some new toys, which we both like because they squeak. There was another toy that I loved—it was a ball that squeaks as we rolled it along the ground. Reuben and I can't play with it when we were together because we squabble. So it was my special toy to play with on my own. But I didn't mind letting Hugo play with it. I have trained Mistress to put bits of treats into the hole in the ball; then when I roll it along in different directions, the bits of treat fall out and I munch them.

Hugo hasn't quite got the hang of this, so if he was pushing the ball around and a treat fell out, I'd be in there. Mistress told me that it wasn't fair, but how would Hugo learn if I didn't teach him. He'll learn to be faster at getting the treat, and will have more fun if I teach him my way. He runs round and round the garden and I try to catch him, which is a lot harder than it seems, for such a little pup he runs really fast. And being so little he can get through places in the garden that I can't. He is a clever wee thing. He chases me too and we roll about. His teeth are sharp, but if I do a very low growl he stops. Until the next time.

Mistress and The One With The Beard were happy we were getting on. It meant lots more cuddles and play for both of us. I still get Mistress all to myself when Hugo sleeps or when we go to what she calls "dog training". How silly she was, it was where I saw all my chums. A nice lady they called Yvonne taught our humans to understand us, and she helped us get our humans trained properly. I preferred to think of it as "human training"—that's much more accurate.

We did have great fun at the human training. Yvonne was very patient with our humans, and explained that if they didn't do what they were told, we dogs would caper about and try to play. She spent a lot of time explaining how we dogs think to our humans. She was a very good trainer and we liked working with her. She obviously understood us well. She explained that dogs use all their senses: smell, hearing, sight and body language. And she was quite right. We might not be able to talk, like humans, but even our bark has meaning—it's just not often understood by humans. I think Yvonne has done a lot of work with dogs and spent a long time trying to understand us. She explained to our humans that even the tone of voice they used, makes a difference. The facial expressions humans use can make communication with us better. If only all humans were like Yvonne. Anyway, we knew she was on our side, and would help us to train our humans properly. And she explained to our humans the importance of giving us treats when they behave properly. I liked the training class, especially when I got to see Reuben and his Mistress. I hope Hugo gets the chance to take Mistress there. Then at least Yvonne will teach us all to train our humans in the same way. That would make life much easier.

I was quite glad to have Hugo to myself to get to know him. Don't get me wrong, I miss Reuben, but if Hugo and I become friends, imagine how much fun it'll be when Reuben comes back and we can all play together. Bring it on.

I used to get to see Reuben at the training, which was fun. We didn't play together because we were concentrating on getting our Mistresses trained. Reuben managed to get his Mistress to pass her Gold Award, which was very exciting. It's something to do with what the humans call "The Kennel Club". My Mistress tried to get her Gold Award too; but she didn't say the right thing to make me go to bed, so I just ignored her. So then we were back to practicing.

We practiced at home too. Hugo was so funny; when Mistress and I were concentrating, he bounced around looking cute, but we just ignored him. He got cross that he didn't get a treat, but I kept telling him that he needed to start training Mistress too, and then she'd be allowed to give him a treat. I thought he was too young to understand. But as I was practicing with her, to get her really well trained, Hugo starting to join in. That was going to make it easier for him once he had the responsibility of taking Mistress to the training with Yvonne all by himself. Mistress was very good and didn't give him anything unless he did exactly the same as me. I hoped she'd pass her Gold Award the next time. She got the hang of sending me to bed and she was very good at it, so I think she might pass.

One evening after doing some extra practice, we went to the training class. Mistress seemed really nervous, and when we got there it was test time. I jumped about a bit to reassure her that she'd do well this time, then she had to show the lady how well behaved she can be for me. I had to get her to stay really still while I laid down and watched her, then she had to go out of the room quietly for a couple of minutes, while I waited to see if she could come back in with no fuss, stand beside me, and then give me a treat. She did it beautifully.

Then we got to go outside and she had to walk very close to me so that the lead wasn't tugging. We walked along the pavement with cars driving by on the road, turned and then walked back to a special crossing place where I had to get her to wait nicely while I sat beside her. She had to wait at the side of the road while I sat and watched her until a beeping sound went off. Then I let her lead me across the road. Then we walked up and down again with her walking nicely beside me, and then we crossed the road again at the special crossing place.

Then, there were a couple of other tests. Like letting her leave me by myself out of sight of her. I had to sit quietly and hope she didn't make a noise while I sat very still. She managed this very well, then—it was the big one—going to bed. She told me to "go to bed"— my basket was at the other end of the hall and because she said it the right way this time, I trotted happily up the hall and sat in my basket and waited to see if she could walk straight towards me and give me a treat. She passed this test, and everyone was clapping because she's got the Gold Award. I was so happy for her; she was just as good as Reuben's Mistress now. Finally, I had her trained. I expect she'll slip up now and again, but I'll just have to keep encouraging her to behave properly.

Maybe I could get Hugo to help me. He helped me train Mistress, and because she was doing so well I even trained Mistress to reward him too. For a little guy, he was learning very quickly about the benefits of getting Mistress well trained.

I think he should keep it going and get Mistress to carry on at the class with him supervising her. Imaging if he taught her how to speak to him properly—maybe one day she'd get another Gold Award.

Imagine having a Mistress with two golds—Hugo and I would be so proud.

Chapter 14

Home From Home

Rufus

We had a very exciting time when Hugo was a young pup. Reuben wasn't staying with us at the time. Box things with handles and wheels came out of the cupboard in the ceiling above Mistress's bedroom. She put lots of things in the box things—"cases" I think she and The One With The Beard called them. He packed some of his stuff in another case. I was a bit worried, what was going on? It was a bit like getting ready for a Special Trip because our dog cage was involved, but The One With The Beard also seemed to be involved, which was unusual. Then Mistress put a lot of our stuff in a case too. I checked with Chip, in case he knew what might be happening. He seemed to think that this happens from time to time. We all go and stay somewhere else for a few days. He told me not to worry.

That sounded quite exciting, so Hugo and I tried to help Mistress as much as we could. Hugo climbed into one of the case things and started rummaging through the clothes to see what Mistress had put in them, but this didn't seem to be the kind of help Mistress wanted. I started collecting all my toys and putting them in the case. I was worried that Mistress might forget to take one of them if we were going away, but apparently this wasn't helpful either. In fact, all the enthusiasm Hugo and I showed just seemed to make Mistress cross, and she shouted at us. Yes. Shouted. Mistress hardly ever shouts, and especially not at us. We climbed into the big dog basket beside Chip and sulked. Chip had warned us not to get in Mistress's way, and that everything would be alright, but it is my duty to help Mistress whenever I can, and Hugo thought the same, so help we would. Besides, Chip was old and smaller than us, so maybe he just wasn't able to help. I thought that I might not even take a biscuit from her now. Chip grunted a very uncharitable "I told you so; now settle down and shut up".

Hugo snuggled up beside me, joining me in a team sulk. A while later, after our sulk had turned into a sleep—it's hard to keep a sulky look up for long as it generally makes me sleepy—Mistress offered us a biscuit each. Hugo, of course, immediately jumped up, forgetting all about the shouting and our sulk. He wagged his tail at Mistress and took the biscuit. Chip took his and, overcome with love for Mistress, I took mine too. She cuddled us all and told us how good we were. I can't resist Mistress; she's lovely.

The very next day, we got up really early. Mistress took Hugo and I for a ridiculously short walk, so something was definitely going to happen. She shut us in the kitchen, leaving us to peer out of the door to the hall where Mistress and The One With The Beard were up to something. The cases were taken out of the house along with our dog cages and our big doggy bed. Mistress came into the kitchen, and clipped our leads back on. Even Chip got his collar and lead on. Now this was really odd. Chip was so old that he only came for a walk if he was in the bag that Mistress carried. I didn't know Chip had a lead. She led us out to the big car, and popped us into our cage in the back. Chip got to sit on her lap, but that's fine. He's the boss, even though he's much smaller than me. We know our place. I love Chip; he's been very good to me ever since I came to live with him. After him having Mistress for so long, it's good of him to share her with us.

We snuggled down in the back of the car. This looked like a big trip. Mistress had put all sorts of things in the back. The folding chairs were there, what looked like a picnic basket, dog towels and our bowls. The dog towels were a good sign because they usually meant that water fun of some kind would be involved. We tried to stay awake and look out of the window, but, as usual, we all fell asleep after a while. It was good having Chip with us, it wasn't often he got to go in the car.

Much later, the car stopped and Mistress came to get us out. Chip was already on his lead, and was wagging his tail. It was good to see him so happy. She put leads on Hugo and me, and let us all have a sniff around beside the car. I knew the smell in the air; this was a bit like the show we went to that was by the sea. I could smell the sea. We all thought this was very good news. I wondered when we'd be able to run on the sand, like we did when we went to the beach with our Cavalier pals Rory, Mikey and Leo. I'll tell you about them later.

Disappointingly, we got put back in the car before we found the sand. We'd only been able to take Mistress for a quick walk, and taken advantage of that to have a leg-lift. Back in the car, I couldn't see out of the window, but I knew we were moving. There were lots of bangs and rumbles, and then the car stopped again.

The air smelt quite different now. We were somewhere inside with lots of other cars very close to our car. Mistress got us back on our leads and out of the car. She carried Chip in the bag, so The One With The Beard took me and she took Hugo. He led us up some stairs with lots of other people. I wondered what kind of house this was. I couldn't believe how many people were crowding around us. I wasn't surprised that Mistress carried Chip; he'd be terrified if he had to walk on the ground. The funny house had metal steps, then carpets, but I could smell the sea very strongly. Then there was a big sound, unlike anything I'd heard before, and the house started to move. Mistress and The One With The Beard sat down beside some lovely people who made a big fuss of us. I couldn't understand why the house was moving. Everyone was being very nice to us, but it was all very confusing.

Mistress took Chip out of his bag and gave him to The One With The Beard to cuddle. She took Hugo and me across to a door, and then we went outside the house. This was really strange. There was a wooden floor outside the house with a railing. Mistress wouldn't let us pee on the posts, but as we peeked through the railing, I could hardly believe my eyes. The house was moving across the water. No wonder Mistress, Hugo and I were all swaying. She knelt down beside us to help us feel safe. This house was something called a "ferry" she said. I snuggled close to her. Hugo was shaking a bit, so she cuddled us in close. I could see seagulls flying around, but had no inclination to jump up to catch them.

I think I could do anything scary as long as Mistress was with me. I know we have to do lots of training with her, to keep her in check, but at times like this, when the world feels very uncertain, I just need her close and then I know everything will be OK. We're a good team, Mistress, Hugo and me. At desperate times like this, we all need each other. Mistress has such a soothing voice. She seemed quite happy with this moving house, that she reassured Hugo and me. Mistress led us back inside. We sat beside her and The One With The Beard for a while. Then Mistress put Chip back into his bag and we all went back down the steep metal steps to our car. I felt a lot better once I was back in the familiar surroundings of my cage, and I think Hugo felt the same. He's usually so bouncy, but even he was quite subdued. The journey obviously wasn't over yet. There were lots of rumbles and bumps again, and the car set off. I could smell the sea again once we'd driven out of the ferry. Then we seemed to be driving along a road.

It wasn't long before we stopped again. This time the sea smell was really strong. We had stopped outside a house. And joy of joys, it was right beside a beach. We ran around the front garden, Hugo and I barked in between sniffing. Even Chip seemed very happy, sniffing and scampering around with us. I couldn't wait to get to the beach, but despite carefully checking every inch of the fence, there was no way out. Mistress and The One With The Beard were laughing at us as they took the cases, our cage and beds, and what smelt like food, into the house. Eventually they let us in to check out the house. They really should have let us in first to check it out before they did. We're meant to be looking after them; after all, we can sniff things so much better, and can sense anything dangerous before they can. Once we had thoroughly checked the house, and jumped on all the chairs, couches and beds, Mistress put our water bowls out and gave us some biscuits. She showed us where our dog beds were, one in the kitchen, one in the lounge and the other one on the bedroom floor, and then she put one of our covers on her bed, and our other covers on the couches, so we knew we'd be allowed on them.

The sun was lovely and warm, so Mistress and The One With The Beard took us out of the gate in the front garden and onto the beach. Chip trotted beside Mistress quite happily while Hugo and I ran and ran down the beach. There was no one else on the beach, just lots of birds—seagulls, crows and great big birds called "swans". Mistress told us to leave them alone. She shouldn't have worried; they were far too big for us to risk chasing. Their beaks looked pretty scary. I wondered how long we'd be here, but I was going to do my very best to catch one of the seagulls. Hugo and I ran through the little waves, which ticked our paws. This was just heaven. Then Mistress noticed that Chip wasn't beside us. She couldn't see where he was. I spotted him right up at the top of the beach, heading for the house. He'd had enough and was going back to the comfort of his basket. I chased after him to show Mistress where he was. She ran behind me, but I got to Chip first because I'm a much faster runner than Mistress. I call it "the four leg advantage". Chip told me that while he enjoyed the beach, he was tired and wanted his bed. Mistress caught up with us and picked Chip up for a cuddle. She carried him back to the house. I had to admire him, he had her so well trained, and she always did exactly what he wanted. I ran back to The One With The Beard and Hugo, and we carried on with the walk.

Here I was, with my lovely family, on a great big adventure. I was the luckiest dog in the whole wide world. I barked and barked loudly, just to let the world know how happy I was.

Chapter 15

Something Mistress Calls "Ring Craft"

Rufus

There was another kind of training Mistress had to do. She called it "Ring Craft". We saw lots of other dogs at Ring Craft. It was a bit like a tiny dog show, but none of the humans got a prize. We got the chance, us dogs, to put our humans through their paces to get them ready for the real shows. And if they behaved well, got us sorted properly on the show table, and walked round the ring, they'd be allowed to give us a treat.

On one occasion I didn't see Reuben there, which was a shame because I knew we'd have fun. As Reuben wasn't there to play with, I lay down and listened to Mistress. It's amazing what a dog can pick up by sitting or lying quietly and listening. While Mistress was chatting, I heard the Crufts word again. It sounded like this was the show to aim for, and that only the best Mistresses could go. It was obvious to me then, that Crufts was the one I'd have to train her for. When I first started taking Mistress to ring craft I used to have to hide under the chair. There were chairs all around the big hall. And there were mats like the ones at the dog shows. They were there for us dogs to walk on, while we showed off our Masters and Mistresses. At first it was a bit scary because I was there with lots of other dogs, some of which were quite big and worrying. When I was little, I got a bit nervous meeting other dogs, but I'm fine now.

I gave myself a big fright one time when Mistress and I had just started going to ring craft. Mistress was busy talking to another human, and not paying attention to me. I was looking around the hall at all the other dogs. I didn't have my usual collar on; it was what Mistress called my show lead. I thought I'd like to go and speak to some of the other dogs. I was feeling brave. We'd been a couple of times, and I didn't feel quite so nervous. Mistress was happy chatting, so I thought I'd do some chatting too. I looked around and saw another dog I thought I'd like to speak to, so I slipped out of my show lead to go and talk to a very pretty girl dog. She had a very fluffy white coat and a very waggy tail. I was so entranced with her that I didn't notice a huge dog coming up behind me. He was a million times bigger than me, and I wasn't at all convinced by his wagging tail. He nudged my back and I got such a shock, I looked around for Mistress. I couldn't see her. In my panic, I spotted the door and headed for it. I knew Mistress's car was out there. She might have left and be in the car. I'd got such a big fright, I wasn't thinking properly. I ran out of the hall to find my car. It was all Mistress's fault, she's supposed to keep me beside her, but she was so busy chatting she didn't see me go and speak to the pretty girl dog.

She ran out of the hall after me, but I was too quick for her. I ran around one of the cars outside, looking for my car to jump into. I couldn't find it, so in desperation I went back to the hall and jumped up on Mistress's chair. I could hear her calling outside for me and the other humans were laughing. Eventually, one of them went outside and told Mistress I'd come back in, so she came back in too. Then— you'll never guess what—she got all cross with me. What a cheek. She was the one that was so busy chatting that she forgot all her training and abandoned me. I just tried to ignore her and got my own back by not letting her show off. I refused to walk properly, and when she was meant to put me on the table, and show how well she could do, I just kept sitting down on the table instead of standing nicely. Another lady was trying to check my teeth and run her hands over me to see how well behaved Mistress was. I also sat down while she tried to walk me round the hall. I had to let her know how angry I was that she'd ignored me and had been cross. I felt it was very unfair that just because she wasn't paying attention, I got the row. I wasn't an expert in training her yet, but with persistence, I'd get her trained. According to all the other dogs I chat with, you have to persist, in order to get your humans to behave.

Eventually she gave up and we went home. I fell asleep on the trip home, although I did try to stay awake so I could sulk some more but I was too tired. Luckily, when we got home, clearly she'd got the message about how I was in the right and she was wrong. I woke up when the car pulled up into the drive. Mistress undid the harness she puts me into when I travel on the car seat beside her, and then she picked me up and gave me a big cuddle. I knew then that she knew she was trying to say sorry. I love my Mistress. That's the thing about us dogs—we never do sulks for long. As long as they let us train them well, we'll be loyal and true to our humans. If we have good humans, we love them no matter what. If they are good and faithful to us, then they deserve to be loved. When we got home from the ring craft that night, all was forgiven as far as I was concerned. As Mistress was trying very hard to make it up to me and I got some sausage with my tea, my world was good. I ate it all to show her that she was forgiven for not behaving at all well at ring craft.

CHAPTER 16

Visiting Gran and the Other Ladies—I like The Coffee Mornings Best

Rufus

I love it when The One With The Beard takes us up the road instead of down to the park. I couldn't understand where we were going the first time he turned the wrong way when I was taking him for his walk. It was exciting. As it turned out it was a good diversion. We went up the road and into a very big house. I met lots of people as well as the one they call "Gran".

Gran usually comes to my house, but I sometimes go to see her house. The first time I went, there were lots of people there. The One With The Beard kept me on my lead in Gran's big house, apart from when I was in Gran's room. She has a lovely bright room, and she can see into the garden from the window. There are lots of feeders outside her window, like Mistress has in my garden, for the birds. Gran can see the birds from the window. She has a room with a bed, a comfy chair, a chest of drawers with lots of pictures on it and another set of drawers with a big vase of flowers on the top.

Apparently, Gran is The One With The Beard's mum. She doesn't look at all like him, whereas, Phoebe, our mum looks just like us. I sniffed around her room when we got there, and Gran gave me a lovely cuddle. I sat on her knee, and I got to snooze under her bed. I wasn't supposed to go on top of her bed like I can at my house. I even got to shred a paper hankie when I found one she'd dropped and I could sneak it under the bed. When Gran dropped the paper hankie on the floor, I think she did it just for me, but The One With The Beard spoilt it and took it away from me when he found me under the bed with the hankie. I couldn't seem to get him to understand that it was our game, not his. Gran didn't try to get it from me, she just laughed.

I often accompany The One With The Beard when he takes fresh flowers to Gran every week. Gran lives with lots of others, and we usually walk down a long corridor to get to meet them all in a big room where they all sat in very comfy chairs and couches. The chairs are in a different place every time we go so that the ladies and gentlemen can chat, doze, watch TV or do other things during the day. They move the chairs depending on the activities the people are doing, which makes it a bit confusing for me. No one seems to sit in the same place so it takes time to work out where the lady who always sneaks me a sweet treat is sitting. She called it a "biscuit", but it tasted much nicer than the biscuits Mistress gives us. If Gran isn't in her room when we first get there, then we go and check the big room. If she was busy doing something else with her friends, we just leave. It was disappointing when that happened, because I get lots of attention from Gran and her friends. I get to sit on lots of different knees and get kisses and cuddles. The ladies all look a bit like Gran, but they all smell different.

It's good fun when The One With The Beard takes Reuben with us to Gran's. Reuben used to be a bit scared of meeting all the people at Gran's house, so he'd keep a firm hold of his toy. The people at Gran's house think it's cute that Reuben holds one of his toys. He's got loads of them, so chooses a different one each time we visit. He drops his toy once he feels more comfortable, but he always holds his toy tightly when we go up for what everyone calls the "Coffee Morning".

Gran's house is full of lots of extra people on these occasions, and the big room is full of tables with lots of things on them. The extra people buy the things, then go to the next room for tea, coffee and scones. Mistress and The One With The Beard come with us and join in. The house is very busy when it's filled with lots of people. We'd let them sit around the tables for their coffee and scones, and, if they are good, we look extra cute and hang around for the scone crumbs. Mistress tells people we're not allowed sweet things, but the other people there are clearly brighter than her and drop bits for us. She's usually so busy blethering that she doesn't notice. We lie down, and then crawl as far as we can on our leads to clear up the crumbs. Really, we are just helping the humans who look after Gran and her friends by doing some of the tidying up.

At one of the first Coffee Mornings Reuben went to, he was so scared of all the people he didn't know, he wouldn't even drop his toy for a tasty sweet treat. I was so busy looking cute, and munching a big bit of scone that had dropped to the floor within my reach, that I didn't notice he'd slipped out of his collar and had sneaked away to the corner of the room trying to escape or hide from all the people. Mistress suddenly jumped up and said loudly, "Where's Reuben—he's slipped out of his collar."

Everyone looked around, including me, my mouth full of scone. He was nowhere to be seen. I was a bit scared, as Reuben didn't know Gran's house nearly as well as I did. I pulled on my lead to try to let Mistress know that if she let me off my lead, I'd find Reuben easily as I'd be able to follow his scent. But she wasn't paying any attention to what I was trying to tell her. She just pulled me back and handed my lead to The One With The Beard. I jumped up at him to see if he would understand, but he just held on to my lead and ignored me. Humans just don't think like us dogs. Who better than me to track down a runaway Reuben? Mistress and some of the other people looked round to see if they could see Reuben. Mistress went in to the next room to see if he was under any of the tables.

Then a voice from the kitchen room shouted, "He's here, I've got him."

And there was Reuben, happy as you like, getting cuddles and a whole scone fed to him while Mistress put his collar and lead back on. Lucky Reuben. I wish I'd thought of that trick. And he didn't even get a row.

Ever since then, when we all go up to see Gran, Reuben is much less scared and spends the whole time trying to get into the kitchen.

When little Hugo arrived, he got more cuddles than Reuben and me put together. He went up as a small pup, so he learnt from the start how good it was to go up to see Gran. When I was a pup, Gran lived somewhere else by herself and The One With The Beard would go in his car and bring her to my house for a visit. That was good fun; I used to get to sit on her knee nearly all the time. She'd sit by the fire and sometimes she'd drop off for a snooze, so I'd just curl up and doze with her. And sometimes she'd stay for a meal. I liked it when she did that; she used to drop tasty bites on the floor for me when Mistress and The One With The Beard weren't looking.

I'm glad Hugo likes to come with us and get lots of cuddles because he looks such a cute puppy. Still, he won't be a pup for long so he might as well make the most of it.

Chapter 17

A Dog in a Bag?

Rufus

We have all got used to having Hugo around. And it is even better when Reuben got his Mistress to bring him over to stay. Hugo learned to treat Chip with a bit of respect. At first he tried to play with Chip the way he plays with us. Chip was not exactly pleased when Hugo tried to catch his tail and bite his ears. Chip didn't hesitate in telling Hugo to stop. If it hadn't been so annoying for Chip, it could have looked quite funny. But I have huge respect for Chip, and know that it's not fair to treat an old dog like that. I think Hugo finally realises that Chip is older, rather than a puppy like him. Hugo was a bit confused because he was the same size as Chip when he arrived and Hugo hadn't seen any other kinds of dogs, so I had to explain that Chip was a different breed to us and wouldn't get any bigger. Chip would grump at Hugo when he got too cheeky, but waged his tail too, so that was good.

When Hugo first arrived, he didn't go out for walks with me. Mistress used to put a light collar and lead on him to walk him around the back garden. I think he was too young to go all the way to the park. He'd probably have got too tired. Then once he was a bit more familiar with the garden, Mistress took him out with us to the park. I remember the first time. Instead of having a lead like me, Mistress popped him into a bag she had to put over her shoulders so that hung down the front of her. Very odd behaviour—I'd never been in a bag before. Wee Hugo sat in the bag with his head sticking out the top and off we went. I got Mistress to let me off the lead as soon as we got to the park because she had walked so nicely beside me. If she didn't walk nicely, I wouldn't let her let me off the lead till we were well in to the park. That's all part of her on-going training. Sometimes she pulls—that's not polite.

Hugo stayed in the bag for the whole walk. I tried to jump up to explain to Mistress that he'd love to run around with me, but all I got was "Down Rufus", as if I was doing something wrong. She just didn't get it sometimes. All the people we met spoke to Hugo first because he was all cuddled up to Mistress, and looking really cute in the silly bag. I felt quite jealous. Usually everyone speaks to me when we were out. At least I could speak to all my doggy friends. With Hugo in his bag, he couldn't meet any of my doggy friends, and they all seemed glad to see me. It's a pity their humans can't see how hurt I feel to be left out. I do love Hugo, but he can be too cute sometimes. Hugo would wriggle about in the bag thing when folk talked to him and Mistress would explain to them that it got him used to being out, but she couldn't let him meet other dogs yet. And apparently it meant I got my walk too. What was she going to do—not walk me because of Hugo? She should really have left Hugo at home; then I'd get all the attention. To be fair to Mistress, she did slip me a treat now and again when Hugo wasn't looking.

I sometimes choose not eat my biscuits when I got home, to show Mistress how annoyed I feel about being left out, but sulking is so difficult with Mistress. She knows just how to take advantage of my good nature with that ear-tickling thing she does.

CHAPTER 18

I love the Vet Sometimes

Rufus

Sometimes, I get to go in the car alone with Mistress. Apart from training or shows, it could either be a trip to the vet, David, or when we go to visit Alfie. This particular time though, the trip was to the vet. Mistress parked the car, got me out on my lead and walked straight past Alfie's shop.

I love the vet, he's all smiley and even though he sometimes gives me an injection, when that happens, I know he'll make it better with a milky biscuit. I love them, and the vet knows it. If he's really gentle with me, I'm happy to let him give me a milky biscuit, and if he's really good, I'll reward him by accepting a second biscuit. It's hard work being a dog; I even have to train the vet.

I felt fine on this particular day, just hungry, because strangely I didn't get any dinner last night, or my biscuits that morning. Unbelievable. But there have been a couple of times when going to the vet has been quite difficult for me. On those occasions, I felt quite unwell and had a sore bottom, especially when I had a poo. I tried not to show Mistress that I felt odd. We dogs feel that showing pain can be very bad for the pack. If we let on we're in pain, the pack could see it as a sign of weakness and abandon us. Or we could lose our status in the pack. I'm the top dog, apart from Chip, so I wouldn't want to lose that place. The sore thing had happened the first time when I was a young pup, and I knew it would get better if I could go to the vet, but I was in a quandary: show I was in pain and risk losing face, or show how uncomfortable I was feeling and hope Mistress wouldn't abandon me. I hoped she'd be OK about my feeling unwell.

Anyway, both of the times when I felt unwell, Mistress eventually realised that something was wrong when I wouldn't sit down. The first time it happened I was feeling a bit wobbly and I hoped she'd understand because although I was getting very sore, I couldn't let her see. She bathed my bottom with some warm water, which was very soothing, then wrapped me in a blanket and put me gently in the front seat of the car. She carefully put my seatbelt on, and off we went. I was very glad that it was the vet we were going to. I let Mistress carry me into the vet's surgery. I felt like biting her because the pain was so bad, but I couldn't do that to her, I loved her too much, and I knew she was trying to help.

David was very gentle. He got Mistress to hold my head while he looked at my bottom. It's very embarrassing, and it was just as well I'm ruby coloured so they didn't see me blush. It was also just as well that Mistress had a hold of my head or I'm sure I'd have nipped David, and that wouldn't be fair. I know he's doing his best to help. Sure enough, I got an injection and two milky bones. Then David gave Mistress a bottle of treats to help my sore bottom. We went home, I slept all the way, but as we got home, I felt a lot better. And she didn't abandon me then or the next time. I'm in a good solid pack.

The second time I got a sore bottom, the same thing happened. David helped me. However, few days later, after the last trip to the vet with my sore bottom, and after all the bottle of treats were finished, Mistress refused to give me my dinner one evening. I tried and tried to tell her I was hungry—after all, I was recovering from my sore bottom. But whatever I did it had no effect. I even pleaded with The One With The Beard to give me my dinner, but he was being as harsh as Mistress. Was this the start of them rejecting me because I'd been in pain and showed it? Chip told me not to be so silly, he gets pains from time to time and Mistress has never rejected him. It was a bit disconcerting though. Chip told me that they'd done this to him once before, then he'd gone to the vet and come home with a sore mouth. He wasn't sure, but thought it might have something to do with the fact that he didn't have many teeth left anymore. Now I was worried.

That next morning I was really hungry. I tried everything to get Mistress to give me something. She didn't share her toast; she didn't take me out for a walk; and the absence of my breakfast biscuits was almost too much to bear. This was clearly the start of me being abandoned. Then, guess what—she put me in the car, in my seat belt and we drove off. Didn't she realise I was hungry, confused and scared that she might take me somewhere and leave me there? Her voice was soothing, but I was too worried and hungry to think straight. I was sure she was taking me away to leave me somewhere else forever.

So there we were, in the car. The journey wasn't too long—we stopped at the vet. This was getting really weird. We never come to the vet first thing in the morning. I wagged my tail at David and tried to tell him I was hungry and that Mistress wasn't behaving at all well, but he picked me up and gave me a cuddle. Then he put me in a cage at the back of his shop. What on earth was happening? I couldn't see where Mistress had gone, but I couldn't smell her any more. So this was it. Abandoned by the Mistress I adore. I was heartbroken, and I started to whimper. David came over and picked up the cage with me in it. He was telling me not to worry, but he was taking me away from my beloved Mistress. Would I ever see her again?

David put me in the back of his car and drove off. Very soon we stopped and he lifted me out of the car and into what smelt like another vet shop. There were lots of lovely, kind ladies there who were all dressed the same. They tried to calm me down. I tried to be brave because I knew that if I showed how scared I really was, it would be seen as a sign of weakness. But I just wanted my Mistress. I got lifted onto a table, bigger than the one at David's shop. There were lots of things around the room. One of the nice ladies held my leg, while another one tickled it with a thing that made a buzzing noise. I looked down at my leg. Some of the hair was missing—what on earth was going on? She kept hold of my leg as David gave me an injection and then . . . well nothing.

The next thing I remember is waking up. I didn't even remember going to sleep. It was most odd. And oh goodness, did I have a sore bottom. It was much worse than the last times, but at least I didn't feel ill, just sleepy and a bit dizzy. I tried to stand up, but my legs were too wobbly. One of the nice ladies opened my cage and offered me a drink. I must have been sleeping for ages because I was so thirsty. She wouldn't let me have as much to drink as I wanted. These humans were behaving very oddly. And why did my bottom hurt? I tried to curl round for a look, but I must have dropped off again.

The next time I woke, I was given a longer drink and was able to stand up. David came in and lifted me out of the cage and onto a table. He looked at my bottom—more embarrassment—and gave me another injection. After a while, my bottom stopped hurting so much so I curled round for a look. My whole bottom was bare. I couldn't believe it. All the hair was gone, right round my bottom. What had happened? The pain I was in must be because all the hair had been pulled out. I couldn't think of any other reason. Surely this was a bad thing to happen. I looked a bit like a type of dog that I saw at the dog shows—ones with bare bottoms and a tuft of hair on their heads and tails. What would Mistress think? But then maybe I was never going to see her again. I felt so sad. The ladies who were all dressed the same were very nice, but how could I tell them that I had a broken heart?

David patted me and told me I was very good. I liked David, and hoped that if Mistress didn't want me any more then maybe I could live with him. I tried to lick his face, to let him know I needed his help, but he just lifted me down onto the floor and put my collar and lead on. I hadn't even noticed anyone taking it off. What was happening?

Then David led me into the front of the vet shop and she was there: my wonderful Mistress, all smiling and waiting for me. I was so happy, I even forgot about my bottom. I wriggled and cuddled into her—I could not have been happier. She'd come back. She still wanted me. She put me down and spoke to David. I heard words like "anal glands" and "operation" and "tablets". So that's why the hair was missing. Apparently I'd had an operation. Well, well, I couldn't wait to tell Reuben about this. I hoped he wouldn't laugh at my bare bottom. Then, joy of joys, we went home. I felt unusually tired when I got home, and although I said hello to The One With The Beard, I was ever so glad that Mistress had put the coal fire on and put my basket close by it, instead of in the kitchen. She even put a bowl of water beside my bed. She gave me a little bit of dinner, but I didn't really feel like eating, which was strange, because I'd been so hungry this morning. Mistress took my dinner away, as I'd hardly touched it, and came back with one of my favourites—scrambled egg. I managed to eat most of it and then snuggled down for a sleep. When I woke up, I had a big drink, went into the garden for a pee, then it was bedtime with Mistress and The One With The Beard. With Chip settled on his rug, Mistress put one of my dog towels on the bed and lifted me up. Just as well, my legs were still feeling a bit wobbly. The towel must be to keep my bottom warm. I drifted off to sleep again, and slept all night.

I couldn't understand why I felt so tired. It's not as though I'd had a big walk or anything. It must be something to do with the operation. I hoped I would never have to have a bare bottom again. I just hoped that Reuben and my doggy friends wouldn't laugh at me. The only thing that worried me slightly was what would happen if my hair didn't grow back. I was going to look a bit silly in the show ring, showing Mistress. It might distract the judge and make it difficult for Mistress to win.

CHAPTER 19

The Big Outside

Hugo

It was the strangest thing. I was allowed to run wherever I wanted in the back garden, but Mistress carried me in a bag thing when she took us out to the park. It meant that I could go out for a walk with her and Rufus, but I couldn't run around the park like Rufus did, which was a real shame. I wriggled when I was in the bag. It was hard to wag my tail when I was in there, so I couldn't greet folk properly.

But I did get to meet all the people who Mistress knew on our walks, even in my bag. They were all very friendly, although I think Rufus got a bit jealous from time to time, as they sometimes forgot to make a fuss of him because they were busy speaking to me. Even though I was in the bag, I felt really safe. It was nice to be close to Mistress and I could look up at her and give her a lick if I wanted to. My head stuck out of the top of the bag, so I could see all the trees, and watch as the branches waved in the wind. The wind ruffled my ears as we walked, which was lovely. I liked that feeling, and just wished I could run around with Rufus. I got to smell all sorts of interesting smells, but I would rather be free to run. I wondered how long I was going to be stuck in the bag. Life could still be a bit confusing to a wee puppy like me.

But today things were different: Mistress put on my collar, and then my lead. That wasn't all that unusual. We'd been practicing with it, and she was getting quite good at allowing me to lead her around the house and garden. Sometimes she'd pull, but if I got her to do it properly, she'd be allowed to give me a treat. Rufus helped too, he was really good with Mistress, but as he kept telling me, it takes a lot of patience to get Mistress really well trained. I tried to be patient with her, but because I am still a puppy, it is hard for me to concentrate on training her properly.

Well, Mistress got herself ready with her jacket and wellies, and my lead was on, and Rufus had his lead on too, which was unusual. He didn't normally get his lead on when I was training Mistress. And then a very scary thing happened. Mistress led us both out of the front of the house and onto the street. I'd never been out of the front of the house before unless Mistress was carrying me in my bag. I was a bit anxious. I've only ever been along the street in my carrier, nice and close to Mistress, where I am able to hear her heart beating next to mine. This was quite different, so I did what instinct told me to do, and sat down. I could tell Rufus was keen to get to the park, and he was a bit cross with me for holding the walk up. But I just wasn't used to this. Everything was huge, and looked much scarier from down on the ground than from up in the bag. Rufus barked at me to get up and walk, but I didn't know what to do. Mistress was on my side, telling Rufus to be quiet. She encouraged me to walk. I stood up and took a tentative step forward. Mistress gave me a treat, even though I hadn't asked her to do anything. I took a few more steps and got another treat. Then I got it. This was another part of her training.

With Rufus at my side, I walked Mistress all the way down the road, allowing her to give me a treat every few steps. She was really good. I took it slowly. It was nerve-wracking training her out on the street. It looked like we were heading for the park, which was exciting. We got to the park, and she let Rufus off his lead. I hoped she'd let me off too, but she was obviously feeling a bit nervous, so I let her walk with me, holding onto my lead, across the park to the entrance to the dell. Rufus ran way ahead, coming back now and again to see how well I was doing with Mistress as I walked with her.

We didn't go far before she carried me for a while, so that we could catch up with Rufus, but when I started to wriggle, she put me down again. I kept her on the lead so that she could practice walking nicely beside me. There were all sorts of smells. I couldn't believe all the different ones, and couldn't help but copy Rufus and do a bit of sniffing. Although I kept my eyes on Mistress at all times. Once I was over the surprise of being able to allow her to walk beside me, it was really quite good fun. Rufus sniffed and lifted his leg all over the place. I don't really get the leg-lifting thing; it looks quite dangerous balancing on one back leg. If I needed a pee, I feel much better just squatting. I had no desire to lift a back leg. Rufus and Reuben both do the leg-lifting thing. They tell me it's what grown up dogs do, but I don't believe them.

We got to the bottom of the hill where there's a bend in the river.

Rufus told me that this was his favourite spot because he'd trained Mistress to throw sticks for him and Reuben here. Just to show me, he got her to throw a few sticks. It looked far too dangerous for me. I'd need to be a lot bigger before I'd try chasing sticks in the river. Then another exciting thing happened when Rufus was splashing about in the water: Mistress unclipped my lead. I stood stock-still. I was on my own, without my lead on. For a moment, I was completely unsure what to do. Then Rufus barked, and I got it. I could have a little snuffle around. Rufus reassured me that Mistress would be quite safe on her own, as long as we kept close to her and followed her if she wandered away. It was great fun running up and down the riverbank and watching Rufus. He was a good swimmer. I ignored Rufus when he barked at me—he was encouraging me to try a little paddle. Sniffing around on the riverbank was just fine for now, thanks. It was all very exciting for a little pup. As I was snuffling around, I wondered if I'd ever need to go back in the bag thing again.

Leading Mistress to the park and getting to run around with Rufus was much more fun.

I enjoyed this walking lark with Mistress, just like Rufus said I would, and she was very good. I thought I was going to enjoy training her. Rufus ran all over the place: up hills, round the trees and he loved jumping in the water. I didn't fancy that much, so once I'd had a good sniff of the water, I got Mistress to stand beside me while I sat down to watch Rufus. She threw sticks into the water; Rufus swam to catch them and brought the sticks back to her. He was such a brave dog; I'm lucky to have him as my friend. He was amazing, being able to control Mistress even though he was in the water. That takes really good training. I hoped I could get Mistress trained like that one day.

We turned around and started to walk back the way we'd come. Mistress picked me up again, which was good; I was feeling a bit tired with all the excitement. At the entrance to the park, she put both our leads on and we walked her nicely home along the street. We got back to the house, with me trotting beside Rufus. I felt quite proud, walking Mistress with my best friend, especially as she was behaving so beautifully. We were so pleased with her that when we got home, we were delighted to let her cuddle us both, and were happy to accept the biscuits she gave us as a reward to her for being so good. I felt quite tired, so after my biscuits, I curled up on the floor in the middle of the kitchen and went to sleep. I didn't even open my eyes as Mistress lifted me up gently and put me in my bed. What a memorable day that was, I'll remember that forever. I drifted off, dreaming of running round the park with Rufus. I was hoping Reuben would come back soon, so we could all go for a walk together. That would be fantastic. A big walk with my two best friends. I really hope Mistress will be just as well behaved when we let her take us out next time.

CHAPTER 20

The Joys of Liver Cake

Reuben

I was with my Mistress in my house, and she was making Liver Cake. Rufus wishes his Mistress could make Liver Cake, because he loves it too. Sometimes my Mistress gives some to Rufus's Mistress so that Rufus can use it for her training. Rufus's Mistress did try to make it once. Just to reassure her, we ate it. It would be rude not to, but it wasn't the same as the yummy Liver Cake my Mistress makes. My Mistress nearly always takes it to the shows. I find it a good reward for her to give to me when I'm showing her. I like black pudding stick too, but Liver Cake is special. I think giving it to me calms my Mistress down and helps her to show off well. The smell of it cooking in the kitchen drives us all nuts. There are eight of us here, so our Mistress keeps us out of the kitchen, but we know what's going on.

It's ages since I've seen Rufus. I hope he's coping OK with wee Hugo. When I left him, he was very unhappy about having a new puppy to stay. We've had a few puppies here. Mostly they go to other homes eventually, and I really miss them, so it was a lovely surprise for me when Hugo arrived at Rufus's house. I really hope they become good friends. It would be great if we could all be friends. Puppies are fun. Yes, they chew ears, and try to catch tails, and jump all over me, but they do sleep a lot and it's great to be able to share their toys when they're awake.

I love my Mistress, and her friends Sarah, Margaret and Ken, but I do like being at Rufus's too. I get anxious when I walk with my pack here. I know I have to guard them, but my Mistress gets upset when I bark at other dogs and people when they get too close to my pack, especially the girls. I love the girls, especially Evie. And Teasle, she's a lovely pup, full of fun. And Daisy. And all the other girls. I also love a girl Cavalier that goes to the dog shows. She's beautiful and I adore her from afar, but I don't often get close enough to say hello properly. She's called Primrose.

I think I feel less anxious at Rufus's because it's just the two of us. Although now I hope it will be three of us, if Rufus takes to Hugo. I'm very lucky having two homes, although sometimes it's a bit confusing. I love my Mistress very much, but Rufus's Mistress is very good to me too. I just get a bit upset when the girls at my home begin to smell interesting. Annoyingly, that's when my Mistress takes me to stay with Rufus. But I soon forget about the girls when I'm at Rufus's. And by the time I get back to my house, the girls smell all back to normal.

The Liver Cake smelt good while it was in the oven, then my Mistress took it out and the smell got even stronger. We all barked like mad. My Mistress shouted at us, but she was laughing too because she knows she makes the best Liver Cake in the world, and we've trained her to share it as soon as it's ready.

Mistress tried to get us to sit while she gave us each a piece, but we knew her too well. We bounced and bounced and barked, and eventually we got the message when she ignored us. Then the magic moment arrived. We each got a bit of Liver Cake. It was still warm. Absolutely delicious. What could I say? My lovely Mistress makes the best Liver Cake in the world. And I love her. And not just for the Liver Cake. She gives me the most gorgeous tummy rubs when I climb on her knee and flop upside down on her lap. And I give her a big face hug and lick her so that she knows just how much I love her.

She wanted to share her special recipe with you; you are only allowed to use it if you send me some too. I feel it's important for you to have an expert to check whether you're making a really good job of it. Please send enough for all my friends here, and of course Rufus and Hugo.

Apparently once this is made and cooled, it can be frozen. This seems quite ridiculous. Another mad thing that our humans think of. Any self-respecting dog would make sure it was all eaten, surely. Be warned—my Mistress has been making Liver Cake for so long, apparently it's in "old" measures—whatever that means.

Lindsey's Luscious Liver Cake

  1 lb. wholemeal self-raising flour
  1 lb. lamb's liver
  3 large fresh free-range eggs
  6-8 cloves of garlic
  4-6 fl. oz milk

Method;

  Pre-heat oven to 170°C or gas mark 3
  Chop or scissor cut the liver
  Slice or press the garlic
  Liquidise these together or just leave chopped.
  Add the 3 eggs and half the flour
  Add some milk to get a good consistency
  Add rest of flour and milk

To Cook;

  Line one large baking tray or two smaller trays with baking parchment
  Pour the mixture in and cover with baking parchment
  Cook in oven for approx. 1 hour

Test as you would a cake—a skewer should not stick, but come out clean

Remove from oven, and remove baking parchment
Place on cooling tray
Once cool, cut into squares and freeze for future use.

Of course, if you're me, or any of my friends, we think it's much better eaten fresh—after going to all the trouble of making it, it's good to share it and use it up quickly. This is the bit of the recipe my Mistress left out:

"Once cool, cut into squares and share with all your dogs. Make sure they've eaten it all within 24 hours".

Why freeze Liver Cake when it's so delicious fresh?

Chapter 21

Is Darlington Ready?

Rufus

It was another exciting trip in the car. Hugo and Reuben were with me so it was all very good. We'd had a big bath and dry the day before, and Mistress had put our cage, trolley and show case into the car, so we knew it was a Special Trip. She'd bought the show case because it holds all our things for the shows. We like it when she takes the case, because once it is opened on top of our cage, it is really easy for us to pinch the treats she packs for us. Mistress knows we like to help ourselves, so she keeps a close eye on us whenever the case is open.

We all went in Mistress's car to see our friend Montie and his Master. I knew this was going to be fun. Montie has a lovely house with what looks like a big garden, but we've never been in it. Sometimes Mistress goes out, and when she comes back she smells of Montie and we sniff her all over. She must think we're stupid, we know she makes secret trips to see Montie without us. And we know she feels guilty because we get a special treat, like black pudding stick, when she gets home. But this time it was good to have Montie with us, even if he was in his own cage. We see him a lot at dog shows, and sometimes we're in the ring together, trying to get his Master and our Mistress good prizes. Montie enjoys this too. He's a lovely dog, and very friendly. Montie told us his Master has won hundreds of prizes over the years, he's a very famous Master.

Is Darlington Ready?

Montie and his Master got into our car. There was no room in the boot with us, so Montie was put in his cage on the back seat. I don't think he minded too much, he is used to travelling on his own, while we three like to cuddle up together. It was a very, very long drive, so we all curled up and slept most of the way. Montie is a Tri-coloured Cavalier, and very handsome. His Master and our Mistress chattered all the way. I don't think they stopped talking once. From what we can gather we're going to a place called "Darlington". It must be a big dog show, because we all got a good bath and dry a couple of days ago and the words Championship and Crufts were mentioned during the chattering, so this might be another step towards "The Big One". It would be so good if we could all go to Crufts together, it sounded so special.

Montie's Master has been a judge all over the world, as far as we can understand. He must be very important so we were glad he is Mistress's friend. But better than that, he was Montie's Master and Montie was our friend. There was nothing more important to Reuben, Hugo and me. We dogs stick together.

Despite all the chattering in the car, we all managed to get a bit of sleep, even Hugo. Sometimes he howls in the car when he gets excited. I think he decided not to howl this time because Mistress and Montie's Master talked so much that he couldn't get a word in. Mistress doesn't talk all that much at home unless she's talking into the little black box she carries around, and according to Montie, his Master is the same. It must be good for them to have a good blether. It's also good for them not to have us constantly training them, they deserve a bit of their own time. But boy, can they talk. If our Mistress and Montie's Master are sharing a room at the hotel, we'll get no sleep tonight.

By the time we got to the hotel, it was nearly dark outside. Mistress stopped the car. We were all desperate to get out. Mistress got out of the car and opened the door to the boot. We all sat and waited for her to clip our leads on. She opened the cage door in the boot and we jumped out because she asked us so nicely. Then we had a good sniff around and a leg-lift. Montie's Master does the same with him. We followed Montie and his Master into the hotel. It was full of people all dressed up. I didn't think everyone there was going to the dog show, they all looked too fancy. There was even a lady that we called "The One in the Big Dress" who had a huge white dress on. Everyone was making a big fuss of her. I wanted to give her dress a sniff and find out more. She spotted us as we dragged Mistress into the hotel. Mistress wasn't behaving because she wasn't walking as fast as we needed her to. The One in the Big Dress came over to say hello. That huge dress was quite scary close up, and Reuben shook his toy at her. Mistress laughed and we followed Montie up the stairs to a bedroom. Sadly, Montie and his Master were in a different room to us, but that was OK, at least Mistress wouldn't be blethering all night.

Mistress put our bedspread on the bed so that we could jump up. She always brings the bedspread because she knows we like to sleep next to her on a big trip, so that we can keep a close eye on her. We have to protect her even more closely while she's away from home. She needs to have us close to her before we go to the dog show, so that she's in good condition to go in the show ring. We had a good sniff around the room and a drink of water and Mistress put some dinner out for us. I'm usually fairly calm on these trips, but for some reason I felt quite restless. I would have loved to explore the hotel; it was full of lots of good smells. When the One in the Big Dress was talking to us, I could smell all sorts of yummy food close by. A lot more interesting than the dinner that Mistress gave us.

There was a knock at the door, so we all rushed to see who it was. Mistress shooed us back. She really doesn't understand that we should answer the door before her in case it's something that might harm her; we need to keep her safe. She opened the door a peep. It was Montie's Master. He came into the room and I seized my chance. I was off. I slipped past Montie's Master and trotted happily back down the corridor and down the stairs. I could hear Mistress yelling for me, but I didn't care. I was going to find that yummy food. She'd never come after me, because she wouldn't want to leave Hugo and Reuben by themselves in the room. Even still, I had better be quick.

I trotted into the big room downstairs and spotted the table. Everyone seemed really pleased to see me. They all tried to stroke me, which was nice. And they spoke to me really loudly. That was nice too, but I wasn't stopping for a chat. One man tried to pick me up, but I was on a mission so I thanked him with a lick and wriggled back down to the floor. The table was in sight and there were some pretty good smells up there. The One in the Big Dress was standing right beside the table. Everyone was now frantically trying to pat me—their friendliness was quite touching, but I wasn't in the mood for socialising just at that moment. I could smell ham. If I could get someone to give me some ham, then maybe I could speak to all these nice folk. Then I heard a familiar voice. It was Mistress, she didn't sound very pleased. I had no idea why. I could easily find my way back to our room. I just needed ham. Then I realised that these people weren't trying to pat me, they were trying to catch me. That was just not going to happen. I darted under the table, which was a great hiding place because it was covered in some sort of material that reached to the floor. I planned to just wait there until Mistress gave up and went away. The cloth moved. I tried to sneak away and found myself in some sort of white kennel, surrounded on all sides, without a door, but right in the middle of it was a pair of human legs. I just sat down with the shock. Where on earth was I? The kennel thing moved and a hand slid under. And you'll never guess. The hand was holding a roll of ham. Yes, HAM. I dived to grab the ham and slid out of the kennel thing. Right into the arms of Mistress. She was laughing with The One in the Big Dress. I hadn't landed in a kennel; I'd been under the Big Dress. Mistress seemed to be doing a lot of apologising, but everyone was laughing—I have no idea why. The One in the Big Dress handed Mistress a few pieces of ham on a small plate. How come she was getting ham, when I was the one who'd spotted it in the first place? Humans could be so unfair. Mistress then carried me out of the big room. The friendly folk gave me some pats as we passed. Although Mistress just shook her head and apologised.

Montie's Master was in the room with Montie, Reuben and Hugo. Mistress spoke to Montie's Master, and then he laughed too. But although this was very odd behaviour, Mistress didn't seem to be all that cross any more, and we all got a bit of ham. I find it hard to understand humans, they just don't think like us dogs at all. Maybe that's why they can be hard to train sometimes.

The next morning we all got up early. Mistress put us in the car along with Montie after a sniff around, a leg-lift and a poo. We'd seen Reuben's other Mistress and her friend Sarah earlier that morning. What fun, we'd all be together. It was very hectic when we got to the show. There were lots and lots of people and dogs, and it was raining, which annoyed Mistress. By the time we'd got to the benches beside the ring where our cage sits, she was soaked. We were fine, all snug in our cage. In fact it was hard for us all to lie down, because Hugo had got a lot bigger since the last show we'd been to. Luckily for us, Mistress seemed to understand this and although she left us for a short while, telling her friend, Sarah, to look after us, she came back with a big new cage, which had a new bit of bedding that made us much comfier. Hugo had found a bit of paper while Mistress was away and happily tore it up. Hugo loves to tear stuff up, and was pleased Mistress left him something to chew. She doesn't usually leave chewable things in the cage, but Hugo reckoned that she'd done it to settle him, and once it was all chewed up, it was another chance for her to practice with the treats. Hugo was very pleased that he'd found something to keep him busy while Mistress was away. He misses her at the dog shows when she goes out of sight, and sometimes he cries and barks. Reuben and I would never do anything like that but Hugo is a bit of a "Mistress's Boy". He sometimes howls when he knows she's in our house, but can't find her. When he does this, Reuben and

I just go back to sleep because we know Hugo has trained Mistress to come and find him immediately. It's a smart bit of training, and not something I'd thought of. It works every time. Once she'd put us into our roomy new cage, she picked up the shreds of paper that Hugo had munched. And then she let out such a cry that everyone around asked her what was wrong. We all sat up and wagged our tails encouragingly.

But as it turned out, from what I could gather, Hugo had shredded what Mistress called the "Removal Passes". This is quite an important bit of paper—it's the bit of paper that she hands in when we leave the dog show, and she can't leave without it. Really, she should be more careful. If it was that important, she shouldn't have left it in the cage with Hugo. My personal favourite is paper hankies, but for some reason, Mistress isn't keen. Anyway, shredding bits of paper is just part of our job as dogs. She eventually managed to get a replacement for the important bit of paper, so what on earth was all the fuss about?

Mistress was very nervous in the ring at the show, so much so, that none of us could get her to behave properly, so she didn't win even one rosette. I felt sorry for her. It wasn't often she went to a show and didn't get any prizes at all. We all gave her an extra big hug and lick while she was getting us back into the car for the drive home. I wondered if I'd put her off a bit by my ham expedition. I hoped not. She must just have had a bad day. We'll need to do a lot more training with her when we get home.

Chapter 22

I Love Primrose

Reuben

We were off to another dog show. Mistress was looking good and we all hoped she'd do well today. We all cuddled up in the back of the car, and for once Hugo wasn't singing as he often does. I think he speaks to Mistress to remind her we're here; although I just don't know how she could possibly forget us.

When we got to the show, I was very glad to see Mikey, Rory and Leo were there too. I like it when our cage is next to theirs; I know them well so I get less anxious when they're near. Their Mistress is always very nice to us, and I like it when she comes to our house, because she loves cuddles as much as Mistress does. I do like to give cuddles. I like to get right up and give big kisses too, although not everyone appreciates that. When Skye comes to the house, she lies on the floor and Rufus, Hugo and I try to wash her face. Mistress tells Skye to get off the floor, but we've got Skye so well trained, she just lies there and giggles.

The show was busy, but not as busy as the really big ones we go to sometimes. Mistress got us out of our cage one at a time for a brush. I think it gives her confidence to do well in the ring if we look good. I know the judge is really looking at Mistress, but I like to look good so that I can show her off really well.

Hugo was first in the ring; he did really well with Mistress. I could see them from my cage, which I really like. It's useful for Rufus and I to see exactly how Mistress performs, so that if she doesn't do well, we can give Hugo tips on how to help her do better next time.

She walked well and stood very nicely. I was delighted when the judge gave her a red rosette. Hugo was really pleased. We love it when Mistress wins, and of course, so does she. Then it was Rufus's turn. As he waited to take her into the ring, one of her friends came over to speak to her. It was Primrose's Mistress. Heaven. I really, really like Primrose. She is a very pretty Blenheim Cavalier girl and absolutely gorgeous. I almost like her as much as I like my first Mistress's girl dog, Teasle.

Primrose pressed her nose against the cage and I gave her a lick. I almost forget to look out for how well Rufus was doing with Mistress because Primrose was so close. I hoped I would be able to concentrate on showing Mistress well while Primrose was around. Maybe I'd get a chance to speak to her properly later, once we'd finished showing Mistress. Rufus came back and it was another good result. Mistress had won a blue rosette. It was not as good as Hugo's red one, but she was very pleased with herself anyway. Primrose had gone, so I could concentrate properly on Mistress when it was my turn. I was a bit upset that Primrose had left. It was hard to pay attention to Mistress with half my mind on Primrose.

Mistress got me out of the cage and gave me a quick brush. I think she does this to calm herself down. It must be quite a pressure going in the ring three times. I know it doesn't really matter what we look like, because the judge is really looking to see how well we show Mistress off, but if it helps her settle in the ring, then that's fine.

It all started very well. Mistress stood nicely, and I thought that the judge liked her. Then she walked very well beside me as all the dogs led their humans around the ring. Then, as we waited to go on the table, I let her see how well I thought she was doing by letting her give me a little treat. She stood quietly and calmly while the judge checked how well she put me on the table. All good so far. Then it was the best bit. I got to show the judge what a good Mistress I have by walking her in a triangle round the ring, then up and down. We do this so that the judge can see how well Mistress can walk from the front, back and side. She had managed well with the triangle, and I was very pleased with her. I turned her to walk up and down—and there she was. Primrose. Right at the end of the ring. The blood surged to my head and I couldn't help myself, I really couldn't. I did a quick slip from my show lead, hoping Mistress could carry on without me, as she was doing so well, and I raced to the end of the ring, but Primrose had gone. I could faintly hear Mistress calling me, but now I was free, I had to find Primrose.

The feeling was completely overwhelming—where had she gone? I ran past dog cages, and lots of people, trying to follow her scent. I even had to avoid the human strangers that were trying to stop me. How stupid were they? A dog on a mission just doesn't give up—didn't they know that. I stopped briefly to try to get my bearings. I appeared to be surrounded by Golden Retrievers, their humans all waved their arms and rushed at me. Now I felt a bit frantic. If I could find Primrose, I'd be fine, but I'd lost her scent. I rushed for the stage where there were lots of dog cages, thinking that maybe she'd be there. Up the steps and over the stage I went, sniffing everywhere. I didn't know why everyone seemed to want to pat me all of a sudden, it's not as if I cared for it right at that time. Strange hands tried to grab me, but they weren't used to my wriggle technique, so I was off in pursuit of lovely Primrose again. And suddenly, there she was, right in front of me. I'd found her. I could see her wagging her tail as I charged up to her and then, horror of horrors, Mistress picked me up before I could say a really good hello to Primrose. How completely unfair. Unfortunately, Mistress knew exactly how to cope with my wriggle technique, and my lead was put on firmly. Oops. I could tell she wasn't best pleased. As I came out of the red fog that had overwhelmed me in my pursuit of Primrose, I realised that the show was in a bit of an uproar. But luckily most folk were laughing, including Mistress's judge. I hoped I hadn't ruined Mistress's chance of doing well. Her face was the same colour as the rosette she won when Hugo showed her, and she seemed to be apologising to everyone.

She took me back into the ring, and I managed to get her to settle a bit. Clearly she needed me there to show her, and couldn't carry on without me. I felt a bit silly. She obviously doesn't show well without us guiding her. It was a tough lesson for me to learn. I have to be with her at all times in the ring, and I can't trust her to show herself. The judge was kind, and Mistress got a yellow rosette. At least she got something. And then she had to go back into the show ring with Hugo to find out who the best Mistress or Master was. This was the next stage when a really big rosette was won. Whoever won this event would be the Best in Show, a really good prize to win.

I apologised to Hugo for unsettling Mistress. I told him to stay with her, as she obviously can't manage unless we stay close to her. That must be why the judges at the dog shows need a dog beside the Masters and Mistresses. It's to keep them in check. I suppose that's why we do all the training we do with them. Hugo did well, but Mistress wasn't chosen as the best. Maybe next time.

We got taken back outside at the end of the show and put into the car. I like this bit at dog shows because Mistress usually finds great places for us to take her for a walk after the shows we go to. We drove for a couple of minutes, and then we saw a lovely big park. Mistress parked the car, and we waited patiently while she put our leads on. Then she was allowed to get us out of the car. After all the fuss Mistress caused at the show, she deserved a good walk. And guess who I spotted in the park with us? Another dog taking her Mistress for a well deserved walk. YES—Primrose. Happy, happy days.

CHAPTER 23

Loving and Leaving

Chip

I'm not feeling well. My sight has been getting worse for a while, and Mistress knows that I get scared when out for a walk, so if I go out now, it's in the dog bag. But I have not been out recently. I'm failing, and although my sense of smell helps me, I don't feel right at all. Rufus, Reuben and Hugo understand, and they are very gentle with me, but Mistress really doesn't understand. I love it when she cuddles me, but it's sore. It's getting more and more painful to move around, and although Mistress gives me honey-flavoured medicine to help, it upsets my tummy. The past few days have been hard. I can't get up or down the steps in the garden on my own. I still sniff about with the boys, but they know it's getting more difficult for me.

I hate not being able to make it out to the garden to poo and pee. Mistress is very kind, but it's embarrassing to have a smelly bottom— even though she gently cleans it to make me feel better.

We've even had to stop our teatime barking game because it even hurts me to bark. The boys know I'm getting to the end, dogs just know this; they're very respectful. I try to pass all that I know to them so that they will carry on well without me. They need to look after the humans. Mistress and The One With The Beard are worried, I know, but I wish I could tell them that it's just my time to go.

The ache in all my legs and back was getting worse, so Mistress took me to visit the vet, David. He was so kind, and looked me over very gently. Even that hurt. I think he told Mistress that it's very near my time, and I'm grateful that he can help her understand. He gave me an injection, which helped relieve the pain a lot. Then it was back in the car. I used to love a trip in the car, but now just trying to keep my balance hurt. But the injection helped, and I curled up on my cushion and drifted off to sleep while Mistress drove us home.

I knew she was very upset when we got home. I've let her be my Mistress for a very long time, seventeen human years, and that has been good for me. I've trained her well, and she will be good with Hugo and Rufus, and Reuben when he comes to stay. I'd love to be around longer, but it's time for me to go.

She put my little bed beside the coal fire that I love so much, and gave me sips of water until bedtime. I love to curl up beside her side of the bed on my sheepskin rug. She gave up trying to make me sleep in the dog basket in the bedroom long ago, and now she understands that the sheepskin rug beside her bed is truly mine.

At bedtime, Rufus curled up not far from me, Reuben curled up beside Rufus, as did Hugo. I knew my friends were with me on what I hoped was the start of that big sleep that I longed for. Mistress wanted me to go in my sleep too. I knew from the way the boys were acting that they knew how I felt; it's just a dog code that humans don't fully understand. I slept.

When I woke in the morning things were much worse. The injection David gave me had worn off and I felt dreadful. Mistress understood though. Before The One With The Beard went to work, he made a big fuss of me even though I knew he was upset and really we were saying goodbye. After Mistress came back from walking the boys, she wrapped me in my favourite blanket. Then she knelt down so that I could say goodbye to Rufus, Reuben and Hugo.

These boys mean so much to me, Rufus helped to cheer me up when I lost my friend Gizmo. I taught Reuben how to respect his elders, and I hope that those two will pass on all that I've taught them to Hugo. He's a good pup. I've enjoyed being his friend.

Mistress put me in the car, and I hoped we were going to see David; he helped last night. I remembered all sorts of things on the journey, like arriving at the house, and meeting Ben. Now that I think of it he looked a lot like Rufus, but he died when I was young. Then I thought of my best pal, Gizmo. He was ill like me. I remembered him letting me know he was near the end, and that he wasn't afraid, just very old and weary. Mistress took him away. Just like she was taking me away now. Finally she understood that it was my time to go.

I remembered my most recent exciting time—a Special Trip—not like the trips the boys go on, I'm sick of hearing about "dog shows". What are they anyway? A lot of fuss about nothing. Mistress never did anything like that with me. Just young dogs showing off their Mistress if you ask me. You can't eat the rosette thing they bring home so what's the point?

No, the big trip we did a while ago was scary, but fun. I got to travel in the car, on a ferry I think it was, and in a special bag Mistress used for Hugo when he was a puppy. And then we stayed in a strange house, which had a beach and the sea. I remembered the sea where I'd even had a couple of paddles. The boys had run about splashing in the waves, but I knew how an elderly dog is supposed to behave. Paddling is fine.

By the time I came back from my memories, we had arrived at the vet. Mistress cuddled me close. The water on her face tasted salty as I tried to give her an encouraging lick. It hurt so much. She took me in to see David. He spoke to Mistress, and she nodded. He gave me another injection, and I quickly felt more relaxed than I had for a long time. Mistress lifted me into her arms and held me gently. She held me close to her and sat down, but she didn't stop cuddling me.

For the first time for days, it didn't hurt, and I relaxed into her arms. I felt floaty and warm. I hope Mistress knew how much I liked this feeling. She carried me back in to see David. He did something to my leg that was tickly, but I didn't care. Then there was another little tickle to my leg. I heard Mistress tell me that she loves me very, very much, and then I went into the deepest sleep. So deep it was black for a while.

I opened my eyes, which are clear now. I saw two wagging tails. I couldn't believe it. My Tibetan Spaniel friend, Gizmo was right there and beside him was my Ruby Cavalier friend, Ben. They were in a big, grassy field with sunshine and trees. And lots of other dogs and people too, I think. And no pain. I could wag my tail and walk with no pain. I could run about and play just like I could as a puppy. I understood from Gizmo and Ben that this is where we come when it's our time: a place of sunshine, shade, comfy beds, yummy food and all the love that our humans send us every time they remember us. This is Dog Heaven.

I'll miss Mistress and The One With The Beard, but I hope they know that now I'm at peace. They have Rufus, Reuben and Hugo to look after them. They are very lucky. And I'm with friends I never thought I'd see again.

Goodbye.

Chapter 24

Goodbye Chip

Rufus

It was not good. Something bad was happening. Chip had been very quiet, and he told us he was very tired. It's been hard for him to get up the steps in the back garden for a good sniff around, even though there are only three steps. Like all dogs, he was trying not to show how much pain he was in. It's not good for the pack position to show pain. I told him he'll always be the top dog as far as I'm concerned. He'd put up with all my puppy ways, and were very good friends now. I had a feeling that Chip may not have long to go. Dogs can sometimes sense this way before humans can.

Mistress took Chip away, and when she came back with him he smelt like he'd been to the vet. Now that was very odd. Apart from my operation, we always went to the vet together. Chip didn't seem to have had an operation. Reuben, Hugo and I were very suspicious. Chip had been much slower than usual, and was finding it difficult to get around. When he came back from the vet, he seemed to be in a bit less pain. Mistress settled him in front of the fire on his favourite dog bed. She looked very sad. Hugo didn't bounce at Chip as he does sometimes; he just laid down near Chip's bed, not too close. We all tried to lie close to Chip, but not to annoy him, just to let him know we were there.

Goodbye Chip

Reuben, Hugo and I looked at one another. We didn't think Mistress realised it, but Chip was dying. We just knew; it's part of our instinct. Even Hugo knew, young as he was. We were going to lose our old friend very soon. Chip knew too. He was old and very tired, and we all realised he'd been in a lot of pain. When he looked at us we knew he was saying goodbye. His look told us that the vet had given him something and it was helping. He slept. All evening he slept. We boys didn't really want to go out in the garden without him, but Mistress shooed us out so we went. We didn't hang about though; we just wanted to be near Chip.

At night, Reuben, Hugo and I usually sleep on our bed, which our humans are allowed to share, but on that night we all wanted to sleep on the floor so that we could be there for Chip on his sheepskin rug beside the bed. As Mistress lay in the bed, her arm was stretched out so that she could cradle Chip's head in her hand. It felt like a long night. When it got light, we knew that Chip was much worse.

Mistress took me, Reuben and Hugo for an early walk, but we stayed close to her. She was very upset and I think she knew by now that Chip was dying. We dogs know that happens, and we just get on with living, but I think humans are different. Mistress was so sad, we tried to get her to understand that this is what happens in life and that she still has us.

Chip was very still when we got back in, and he didn't come to meet us. Mistress forgot to give us our biscuits, but it didn't matter as none of us felt like eating.

She picked Chip up and cradled him in his blanket. She looked down at us with water in her eyes. She knelt down to let us see Chip. The water on her face tasted salty as we licked her to let her know we care. We all said goodbye to Chip. We all know he won't be back. He said his goodbyes to us, and passed the job of looking after Mistress fully onto us. It's a big thing when the pack leader dies, but it's up to the dogs left to carry on. Chip told Reuben and me to share the task. He said that as brothers, we should be equally responsible for

Mistress, and that Hugo should help us. He told us how much he loved Mistress, and how kind she'd been. I didn't realise until that moment that Chip had never been to a dog show; he was very proud of how well we had done showing Mistress. Being with our friend as he was dying was very humbling. And a very big privilege. We all, including Chip knew that his difficult time would pass, and it would be up to those of us left behind to help the Mistress carry on. That's what the dogs that are left do in honour of all the ones that have gone on before—they carry on with pack duties. We sat quietly when Mistress and Chip left the house.

I felt very sad about Chip dying. We all were. Mistress kept cuddling us when she came back alone, and her face tasted all salty when I gave her a kiss. I thought back to when I was a pup. Chip was so good to me even though he was old when I arrived. He wouldn't play, but I enjoyed our barking sessions while we waited for our dinner.

Goodbye Chip.

CHAPTER 25

They're Not Dogs—
So What Are They?

Reuben

Mistress seemed to be building us a house in the back garden. I wasn't sure what she was up to. Surely she doesn't want us to live in the garden. We all tried to help her, but she didn't seem to want our help. Rufus retreated and laid down on the grass to watch her. Hugo was just bouncing about, but he was still just a puppy. I sat as close as I could to Mistress without making her shoo me away. The garden house had walls and a roof. Mistress put sawdust, like they have at some of the dog shows, inside it. Then some stuff that smelt like old dried grass went in. She chatted to us while she worked; she told us that the grass stuff was "hay". I tried tasting some, expecting to be told off, but Mistress just smiled at me and told me to go ahead. I tried to chew the hay, but it tasted terrible, so I left it alone.

Once she'd finished building our new garden house, I tried to get into it to explore, but she wouldn't let me. Instead, she put a fence around the house. There was a small gate, but she shut us out of there too. It was most odd. She put a container inside the house, which smelt like it had water in it—so it was clearly meant for us. She put another bowl in, with food that looked like the small dog food kibble that we get fed. She offered us a bit of it, but again it tasted horrid. I hoped she wasn't expecting us to eat this stuff. Rufus was now lying sleeping in the sun, apparently not bothered about the carry on. Hugo had given up too; he slept beside Rufus. But I was a bit alarmed by all of this. I don't like new experiences; they make me feel quite anxious. I wished I was more like Rufus.

I went to get one of my toys. I chose a fluffy, stripy ball. I held it while I watched Mistress. Holding one of my toys makes me feel a bit better. Mistress saw that I was holding my toy, and bent down to give me a cuddle. I'd trained her to notice when I feel a bit worried, and she usually cuddles me. I felt better, but would be happier when I knew what the new house was all about.

Mistress called us all into the big house and closed the back door. Then she took our dog cage, which sometimes goes in the back of the car, outside the front of the house. We jumped up on our chair by the front window, to see what she was doing. She put our dog cage into the car. We haven't been in this cage since Hugo arrived, so it would be quite a squash for the three of us to get in it now. Usually it just sits in the hall for us to retreat to if we need some peace and quiet. She took the dog rug out of the cage, which would make it a bit uncomfortable for us to lie in. Whatever was she playing at? We all barked and I got my toy and gave it a big shake. We must be going on trip. This was good news, and we all forgot about the mysterious house in the garden.

Mistress had the cheek to leave us shut in the kitchen, and go out by herself. We really hadn't a clue what was going on. Surely she wasn't going to get another dog? I looked at Rufus and I could see he was as confused as I was. We didn't need any more dogs to spoil our gang of three. We didn't mind going for a walk with other dogs sometimes, like Rufus's friend Alfie, or Montie when he came to stay, but we wouldn't want another one here forever. I knew Mistress was very sad that Chip has gone, but I thought she was happy with the three of us. Her "Golden Boys" she called us. I held my toy tightly and sat and waited in my basket.

We didn't have too long to wait before we heard Mistress's car come into the drive. She brought the dog cage through the house and straight into the garden. Then she came back into the house, and let us out of the kitchen door. We all rushed out to see what was in the cage. She picked up the cage before we could really work out what was inside, and carried it with its unknown contents through the gate in the fence she'd made around the garden house. And we were not allowed in beside her. She was talking to us all the time, but it was hard to concentrate on what she was saying because we were so desperate to find out what she'd brought home. Surely if this were another puppy, she wouldn't expect it to live in the garden. I had to admit, there were no puppy smells coming from the cage, just something I couldn't work out. Mistress sounded very happy so it must be something good.

Then we got the surprise of our lives. Out jumped three big birds from the cage. Now I love birds, and personally make sure that there are never any wood pigeons in the garden whenever I can. I've never really got close enough to sniff a wood pigeon, but I'd love the chance. We all chase the gulls and the crows down the dell, but so far none of us has ever managed to catch one. I don't bother with the little birds in the garden, because I know Mistress puts seeds out for them. Hugo loves to chase the gulls on the beach when we go there. I remember the time we all went to the beach with our Cavalier friends Rory, Mikey and Leo.

We all raced down the beach and jumped about in the waves. Our Mistress and our friend's Mistress laughed at us. I think they felt very proud to be owned by six lovely Cavaliers. Lots of people tried to speak to us, but we were very busy sniffing and splashing through the rock pools. Rufus was busy chasing a crow on the beach. It kept flying and landing just ahead of him, and he couldn't catch it. He got much further ahead than us and was so busy trying to catch the crow, that he didn't notice that it had changed direction and flown low over a big rock pool. Rufus jumped to catch it and of course it flew off, but he landed in the rock pool and had to swim out. He got such a fright that he ran straight back to Mistress, spluttering and shaking his head to get rid of the salty taste of the sea. He didn't do any more crow-chasing that day. We all got lovely and wet and sandy, but our Mistresses didn't seem to care. We even let them share their picnic with us because they had behaved so well and let us all run about together.

The birds that Mistress had brought home weren't crows, or wood pigeon, gulls, or ducks. We sometimes see ducks swimming on the river in the dell. Even if we jump in the river, we still can't catch them. They cheat and fly off or swim away. The birds in the garden pen looked like nothing I had ever seen before. They had flappy wings but didn't seem to fly. They had golden eyes, black and green feathers, and a funny red thing on top of their heads. It was very exciting. I couldn't wait until Mistress let us in beside them. Then maybe I'd have a chance to catch one. I could tell that Rufus was thinking exactly the same: let us at them. But Mistress clearly had other ideas. She shut the gate of the pen behind her, leaving the birds pecking around their pen and exploring the garden house. Clearly this was a house and area for them—not us. She patted us all, and Rufus and I went over to the pen to say hello. Hugo wasn't so keen, especially when one of the birds tried to peck him when he put his nose against their wire fence. Mistress picked him up and told him not to worry and that these were hens. She put him down and he trotted back into the house.

Rufus and I went up to the fence, but the hens were too busy pecking away to notice us. We decided that we'd chase them at the first opportunity. We looked at each other. It was a deal.

The opportunity came after not too long. Mistress came home, and let us out in the garden as she usually does. There had been a lot of snow, but it was melting so the grass was slippery. I ran out first. At the same moment, Mistress and I realised the hens had escaped out of their pen and were all together at the back of the garden. This was my chance. Mistress yelled at me, but I decided not to hear her. More accurately, there was no way I was going to stop, at least one of those hens was mine. I ran across the wet grass and then realised that rather than run away, the hens fluffed out their feather and wings and the "Boss" one was heading straight for me.

This was not part of the plan at all. Birds were meant to fly away, not go for a full on attack. Whose garden did they think it was? Sure, when we were shut in, Mistress let them out to get a run in the big garden, but the big garden really belonged to Rufus, Hugo and me.

I tried to stop; the sharp, yellow beak that was heading swiftly for my nose was to be avoided at all costs. But the grass was wet, and although I tried really hard to stop—I even tried to sit down—I skidded right into the path of what was clearly a very cross hen. I shut my eyes, but it didn't stop the pain of a very harsh peck, right on the top of my head. Ouch. I turned tail and ran straight back to the house to tell the others NOT to go near the hens. Those beaks really meant business. Rufus and I had watched them demolish the corn on the cob that Mistress would tie to their pen in the evenings. It would be gone in a couple of minutes, so we'd seen their beaks in action. It was not at all funny when their beaks were aimed at me. Mistress had the cheek to laugh, but Rufus got the message and Hugo was nowhere to be seen, clearly he was hiding instead of sticking up for me.

From that day on we shared the garden with the hens, each respecting one another's space. I still chase the wood pigeons away. But there is no way I'd go near the hens. Hugo refused to go out in the garden for a few days after the hens had a go at me. He was still a puppy at the time, and Mistress had to work hard to help him understand that they would keep clear of him. Once us dogs and the hens came to a truce, the cheeky hens even came inside the house through the back door if Mistress left it open, and pecked up the dog biscuit crumbs we'd left on the rug. On a couple of occasions, one hen even tried to pinch one of my biscuits from under my very nose. I still didn't argue. I'd learned my lesson. Respect to hens. Never again, no way. Hens are clearly not to be chased. All I needed now, if one of them got too close, was a good shake of one of my toys.

Chapter 26

A Waggy Tail then Down in the Borders

Hugo

I remember the day that Mistress took me out on my own in the car. Sometimes she did this—took us each out, one at a time. We all like the trips we go on together, but when Mistress takes us out alone, we know we have her all to ourselves for a while. Then when we get back, we can share our adventures.

Mistress and I drove to the park that we usually go to all together with Skye. It has a part that we're not allowed into, full of things that Skye can jump onto, swing from and climb. It always looks like good fun, but we would be left outside at the gate. That was a bit unfair on us dogs, because we all wanted to look after Skye, and didn't feel we were doing it properly if we couldn't be right beside her.

On the occasion when Mistress took me by myself, I hardly recognised the park. There were lots and lots of people, nearly as many as we see when we go to the dog shows, but this wasn't a dog show. There were a few dogs, but no cages, and a lot more humans than dogs. I could smell food, and there were lots of things in all the tents, but most of them didn't smell like the things I smelt at the dog shows. Lots of humans stopped to talk to me, and I thought they were telling me how good my Mistress looked. At least that part was a bit like the dog shows.

After walking around for a while, looking in the different tents I got to take Mistress into a ring, a bit like a dog show. I wasn't sure what was happening there. I didn't get to walk round with Mistress; she just talked to me in the voice she uses when she's playing with me. My tail hadn't stopped wagging all the time I was out with her, but when she talked to me like this, it went even faster. I was completely confused. I was with lots of other dogs, showing their humans, and all the dogs were wagging their tails too. Big dogs, little dogs, dogs like I've never seen before, what was going on? There was no table to stand on, no walking, just three lovely ladies looking at Mistress. She seemed to be encouraging me to get all excited, in which case she would never win, because she'd get too excited and she'd blow it. We both know that to win a prize she has to stand nice and still.

I was trying to get the wagging under control to try to calm her down, but it wasn't working. I could feel my tail wagging faster and faster. Reuben and Rufus would be so disappointed that I couldn't keep Mistress under control at this strange dog show. And then, amazingly, Mistress got a prize. This was the weirdest dog show I've ever been at. The lady judging didn't hand the rosette to Mistress, instead she pinned the rosette to my collar as if it belonged to me. Lots of people patted me and told me how good I had been. Some of them seemed to think that my prize has nothing to do with Mistress, but more to do with my waggy tail. How silly. It turned out that Mistress had taken me to the "Art In the Park" occasion at our local Spylaw Park; it wasn't at all like the dog shows we usually go to. Apparently, my waggy tail won me my own prize. How odd humans are at times.

I had fun that day, but I really enjoyed another show, further away. It turned out to be really special. We all went off on another Special Trip, Rufus, Reuben and me, and it looked like a big one because

Mistress had packed a big picnic, and I think she packed biscuits for us too. It was a beautiful day, and we were so excited. We were all jumping about so much that Mistress put us in our cage in the back of the car while she put our cage, trolley and show box on the back seat. Reuben was shaking his goose very hard and Rufus had his glove so we were all ready to go. Mistress was in a very good mood. I thought it would be a good trip. If she stays like this, I thought she might get a win. I was so excited. I hoped I wouldn't upset her in the ring. Sometimes I just can't help myself. I'm just so proud to be showing her off, that I can hardly keep all my paws on the ground. Rufus and Reuben wagged their tails, but they were not as good at it as me.

This trip took quite a while, so every so often I spoke to Mistress just to let her know I was thinking about her. Sometimes I would yowl at her quite a lot, and then she would speak back to me to tell me that we wouldn't be long. She tried to encourage me to be quiet. But today I was so happy that I spoke to her quite a lot. Rufus and Reuben didn't do this; they knew it was my job to let Mistress know we were thinking about her.

Once we got to the show, I realised that it was a big one. I was hoping to see the Master I had before Mistress. He's a lovely man, and my mum still stays with him. My sisters, Jenny and Lucy stay with him too, and it would be fun to see them as well. I thought Mistress might be expecting to see him too.

We got out of the back of the car and jumped into our cage. This was going to be a show in the sunshine. It meant we had to walk on the grass in the show ring, which could be a bit distracting for us. There are often interesting smells in the grassy ring and we have to concentrate on Mistress. If we get too distracted, we might not pay attention to Mistress and she wouldn't show well for us. I hope we will all get a turn of showing Mistress today; I like it when we do.

Then we saw our doggy chums and our cage was put beside theirs. Mistress covered our cage to shade it from the sun and put a whirly thing on the outside of the cage. This had something inside it that spins round and round and keeps us lovely and cool, however hot it is outside. We got a stretch of our legs, a leg lift and a drink. Mistress got us out of our cage one at a time for a quick brush. We'd had a big bath a couple of days earlier, and a big brush last night, so it was just a wee brush before we took her in. All this brushing could be a bit dull, but we all understand it is part of keeping Mistress settled. Rufus reckons it takes her mind off being in the ring. It keeps her calm before she is in the limelight, so if she's happy, then we are.

My old Master wasn't there, and Mikey's Mistress seemed to be telling my Mistress that he wasn't coming. That was disappointing; I love to see my sisters, who live with him. It seemed, from what we can gather, that my old Master is somewhere called "hospital". I wondered if that was a different dog show.

Reuben was first in with Mistress. I couldn't see how he was doing from where our cage was, but when Reuben came back, he was wagging his tail, but shaking his head. This was not good news. Reuben picked up his toy when he got back into our cage. He didn't get Mistress to behave well enough to get a prize. Rufus was nervous now because it was his turn. I hoped that maybe Reuben had got Mistress settled enough for her to perform well with Rufus. I wished I could have seen them in the ring. It's so annoying at the big shows when our cages are too far from the ring to see what's going on.

Mistress got Rufus out of the cage and off they went. It felt like forever until they were back. Good news. As Rufus came towards us, his head was held high, and his tail nearly wagged off. Mistress had got a third prize rosette. And she seemed thrilled. Reuben was relieved that she'd settled down. Back in the cage, the big boys had a stern word with me. I had to do well, and not skip about. I had to keep Mistress looking at me at all times. She had to walk at just the right pace for the judge to like her. She was only allowed to give me a treat if she did well. On no account should I accept the treat unless she was behaving. No pressure then. I know I've heard this from them before, but I know how excited I get sometimes, so they have a point. If I don't concentrate on Mistress one hundred per cent, I would put her off.

Apparently, Mistress put me in the wrong class, and the only one she could take me into was the one with all the dogs that are really experienced at handling their humans—these are the humans that have done the most winning, so much winning, in fact, that this is the only class they're allowed to go into. Definitely no pressure then. And Rufus and Reuben also think that my old Master will be talking to Mikey's Mistress, on the box thing she puts to her ear, the mobile phone, while I'm in the ring, to let him know how Mistress get's on. I told Rufus and Reuben that I was not sure I could cope. Rufus did his very low rumbly growl to warn me not to let on to Mistress that the pressure was on. She didn't know what was at stake. Mistress told Rufus to stop growling. Little did she know just what all those growls and barks meant between us. Just as well probably.

Mistress got me out of the cage and put on my show lead she uses in the ring. I think it must be her favourite lead because it's red. I hoped it was her lucky lead today, and that she would do well. All her friends were beside the ring when we went in. Just as Rufus and Reuben said, Mikey's Mistress held the little box to her ear and was talking to someone. Humans do this a lot. Maybe it's because they can't bark. She was talking to my old Master to let him know how Mistress performs. In we went.

Mistress seemed to be enjoying herself. There were only three of us in the ring all showing our Mistresses. These are Mistresses that I've seen before; they do lots and lots of winning. They must be two of the top-winning Mistresses ever. The first two went round, and then it was my turn. I desperately tried to ignore the amazing smells in the ring. This was so hard, but I didn't take my eyes off Mistress. I would love her to get a red rosette today; I thought she was doing so well. She lifted me onto the table, and then stood really nicely, so I allowed her to give me a treat. So far so good. Then she lifted me off the table and we walked in a triangle, then up and down the ring, so that the judge could see how well she walks. She did quite well. The judge looked at all the Mistresses, and what a disappointment, My Mistress was third. And I thought that she had done so well, but obviously the judge thought the other two Mistresses were better than mine. Everyone clapped when Mistress got her yellow rosette, and I barked loudly to let everyone know that she should have done better. Even though the other two Mistresses beat mine, I knew I'd be taking the best Mistress home with me.

We walked out of the ring—and what a welcome we got from all Mistress's friends. You would have thought she'd won. There were cuddles for her, cuddles for me—goodness knows why, we were last after all—and everyone was laughing. From what I could gather, Mistress had just won something called her "Stud Book Number", whatever that was. Her friends even got her a big rosette with it printed on it. And she wore it for the rest of the day. Rufus and Reuben didn't know what it meant either when I told them about it back at the cage, but Mikey in the next cage told us that it's something all the humans want. They put these numbers into a special book. He didn't know why. But Mikey did know that it means she can go to the huge dog show the humans call Crufts. Usually, humans have to qualify every year. So now our Mistress can go to Crufts forever with me because I was showing her when she won. Of course, we'd all heard of Crufts, but we now realised that this was the big dog show that all humans aspire to go to. It was the show that all our Mistress training and showing had been leading up to. It would be lovely to see how she gets on at a HUGE show. Then we all got biscuits and some of the rewards we allow Mistress to give us as we train her. She was certainly delighted with whatever had happened. It's all really puzzling sometimes. But if Mistress is happy, then we are.

Everyone was congratulating me, but we knew our Mistress had done all the hard work. Our humans can be very strange at times.

CHAPTER 27

Going to Kennels

Rufus

There was something very odd going on in our house. I thought at first we were going on a holiday, like the one we had when Chip was still here. But this was too strange even for that. Mistress had been filling bags and boxes with everything in the house. They almost filled a whole room. She'd never fit them in the car. There had been lots of people in the house helping her. At this rate, there would be nothing left to even sit on. We kept trying to help her but she just shooed us away. We got all our walks, our biscuits and dinner as usual, but we couldn't work out what was happening. Mistress seemed to be in a good mood, but she was very busy. She was not too busy to brush and cuddle us. We all snuggled up together on the couch in the evenings, but she was so tired that she often fell asleep.

I knew something was troubling her, but none of us know what. We all just tried to stay as close as possible to her. What Mistress often forgets is that we dogs pick up on when our humans have problems. We knew she was sad when Chip died, we know when she's happy or when she's done well at a show—we just pick up on a lot more than she realises. I sometimes think that our humans don't realise how much we dogs understand. We're used to taking cues from our dog packs. We know when there's something wrong with each other, just by the way we sit, stand, hold our ears and tails; there are all sorts of signs that are far too complicated for humans to understand. We may not understand all the words humans say to us or to each other, but their eyes and bodies give them away much more than they realise.

Mistress seemed to be by herself a lot at the moment, we didn't see as much of The One With The Beard as we used to, he just popped in to see us, rather than staying with us. That was a shame, because we love The One With the Beard, but if that was what Mistress wanted, we were happy with that. Sometimes she seemed sad, but we just got a toy and encouraged her to play, and as usual, if she played really well, she could give us a treat. Hugo liked to give her a full on face hug. I liked to do that sometimes too, but Hugo took it too far sometimes. He even jumps right on her head to wake her up. He's young yet. Reuben likes to cuddle her too, but his cuddles involve as much licking as he can get away with. I usually wait till Reuben and Hugo are asleep, and then I can get a good cuddle with Mistress all by myself. Those are the times when I remind her how good it can be when it is just me there. Don't get me wrong, I love Reuben and Hugo, but sometimes it was just grand to get Mistress to myself. I would snuggle my head right into her neck and she'd hug me and stroke my tummy.

There was definitely something going on at this time though, because Mistress could be happy and sad in a short space of time. We were all trying to keep as close to her as possible, so that she knew that whatever she did, we were happy. Just as long as we were with her. She was on the mobile phone a lot.

Then one day, a very strange thing happened. Mistress got up early. She didn't have breakfast, so we missed out on our usual piece of toast. We got our walk, then our biscuits as usual, and then she put lots of our toys, biscuits and treats into a bag and put us in the car. It couldn't be a dog show, because there was no cage, trolley or show box. And we hadn't had a bath, but we did have a big brush the night before. It couldn't be a walk in a different place, like walking with Alfie, because she wouldn't pack biscuits and toys. It wasn't a holiday, there was no case things or dog beds, and so what exactly what was going on?

Reuben gave his toy a big shake, because he was anxious. I tried to tell him to trust Mistress, but he hates anything out of his routine, so I just sat really close to him in the car. Reuben can be quite full on, but deep down he's a real softie who gets worried quite easily. I know he's a few minutes older than me, but sometimes I feel like the big brother. I'm able to be calmer than him, but I know that if I stay really close to him, he'll be reassured. Hugo, of course was just bouncing. He thinks everything is a huge adventure and even gets over-excited about the walk we get every day, there's no curbing his exuberance. I often wonder if he'll ever calm down. But that was just Hugo, and we loved him dearly. I wondered if we had all been like that as puppies, but Reuben and I can't remember. Hugo bounces all the time that he's awake. He's the one who usually wakes up Mistress. He's the one who barks the most before a walk. And he's the one who still demands to be played with. Even when she's sitting quietly, he just has to shake his toy at Mistress to cajole her into a game. She always gives in, and then Reuben and I know we can join in too. One of our favourite games is where we each chose a toy, and play tug-of-war with Mistress; then we let her take those toys and we sit nicely while she tries to hide them where we can't see them. She has never won this game. She really doesn't understand the strong sense of smell we dogs have. Even if she hid the three toys in the same place, we'd bring our own toy back to her. She knows she's lost and she knows the forfeit is a treat. We love letting Mistress play with us.

Mistress got into the car on this occasion and we began our journey. We'd not gone that far when she stopped, and opened the boot of the car. We all sat nicely after getting her to tell us to—all part of her on-going training; and then we let her put our leads on. Once we had got her to stand nicely, we let her encourage us out of the car. This was a new place. And it smelt totally of dogs. But I was almost sure that it wasn't a dog show. Mistress led us into a room and surprise, surprise, there was Montie's Master. But Montie didn't seem to be there. We were all a bit confused. Mistress chatted to Montie's Master and gave him the bag with our toys, biscuits and treats. We heard the word "kennels". Is that the name of the place we're visiting? Then a really nice human called "Colin" took our leads from Mistress and led us away. We were so curious that we didn't even have time to say a proper goodbye to Mistress. It must be OK; she would never give us to someone else unless they were a friend. We'd never met Colin before, but he smelt good and we could all sense that he liked dogs.

He took us to our kennel. There were lots of them side by side in rows. Each kennel had a cover where our beds and toys went and a run attached where we could eat our food and biscuits, have a drink from a bowl and stretch our legs. There was fencing round each kennel and run and a door. We all went in together, but we could see and hear other dogs. I wondered how long we'd be here. We wondered when Mistress was coming to see this place; we'd love to show it to her. I did worry, just a bit, that she might not come back, but with Montie's Master here, I knew we must be safe.

CHAPTER 28

Is This Another Holiday?

Rufus

We'd all just finished our breakfast biscuits and had a brush. We were still living in this kennel place. It was very nice, although we did miss our Mistress. Colin gave us our food and took us for our walks. He even had a play with us, so Reuben, Hugo and I have decided he's a very good human. We wagged our tails like mad when we saw him. Every day we wondered if Mistress had left us there forever, and wondered what we'd done to deserve that. I tried to tell Reuben and Hugo that Mistress wouldn't leave us. But secretly I wasn't sure. There had been a lot going on at home, and I did worry about Mistress. At times she hadn't seemed like herself. Sometimes she was really quiet. We did miss sleeping on our bed, but I was sure we'd find out what was going on soon.

Every morning I hoped Mistress would come to wake us. We don't really mind who comes to see us in the mornings, we're just happy to see someone. We hear and see lots of other dogs. Reuben was a bit worried at first, because he gets a bit anxious around dogs that he doesn't know, but Hugo and I told him not to worry, he was safe here. And he had his toys to shake when he's worried. I was thinking we'd had about four sleeps here. I hoped Mistress would come soon to tell us why we were here.

One morning Colin came in to see us, as he does every day, to put our leads on. We thought he must be taking us for a very early walk, but instead of heading over to the big field where we could run about with our leads off and check out which other dogs had been there, he took us down a different path. And look who was there to meet us. IT WAS MISTRESS. We all pulled like mad to get to her. We were being so bouncy that she didn't know who to say hello to first. Mistress didn't usually like us jumping up at her, but today she was so happy to see us. She just wanted to cuddle us all together. Hugo was absolutely beside himself with glee. He'd found it very hard to be away from Mistress, and being much younger than us, I thought he'd missed her more than Reuben and I had. Mistress chatted to Colin and we got into the car. I hoped we would go straight home; I couldn't wait to run around the garden.

After what felt like a long time, the car stopped. This didn't smell like our home. There were lots of new smells. The hens were here somewhere too. Mistress led us, still on our leads, into a big house. She kept us on our leads while she showed us around. I could hardly believe it. All out furniture was here. All our chairs and couches; our dog beds; the bed we let Mistress share with us at night—everything.

We ran about once Mistress let us off our leads. The One With The Beard wasn't here, but we'd not been seeing too much of him lately. Mistress seemed very happy though. I had a feeling we were going to be here for a long time. The hens were in the garden and we ran all over, exploring and checking out the many new smells. I could smell a river very close by, which was good news, and there were lots of huge trees and bushes outside the garden, so maybe there would be lots of walks too.

Life was always an adventure with Mistress around. She's so lucky to have the three of us to look after her.

CHAPTER 29

Just Another Cavalier Club Show

Rufus

We were back at another dog show. One of the kinds I really like. It was all Cavaliers here, and best of all, lots of girls. We like the girls, although I thought that Reuben was the only one out of the three of us that knew exactly why. He told us that he'd had special fun with girls, but we weren't sure what he really meant and he wouldn't tell us the details. He said that polite boy dogs don't tell.

Mistress and her friends seemed to think this dog show was a special one. Apparently it was a Championship Show. Now we'd heard this term before quite often. We were getting used to this now. We knew there were all sorts of shows, but it seemed that the Championship ones were the ones that really mattered. Hugo did so well with Mistress at the Border Union Championship Show, even though she only came third, that Mistress was going to get to go to Crufts. Everyone talks about Crufts and I wondered if we'd all be allowed to go with her or just Hugo. We'd love to see how she gets on. Anyway, Reuben and Hugo had both been in with Mistress, but she'd been so anxious that there was nothing they could do with her. She didn't get any prizes, so it was all down to me.

She got me out of the cage, popped me on top of it, gave me a quick extra brush, put my special lead on and then off we went. I took her into the ring, and I could feel how nervous she was. It's funny how I can feel right down the lead if she's nervous or excited. I had to keep calm or she'd mess this up too. I gazed up at her as we took our place in the ring. My eyes were begging her to "stay calm". She stood very nicely so I took the chance to have a look at the competition. I couldn't believe it. There must have be sixteen other Masters and Mistresses there, with Cavaliers of all colours. There are four colours of Cavaliers: ruby ones, like Hugo, Reuben and me—we're a lovely rich, red colour and the same colour all over, although I have a tiny bit of white on my chin, which makes me very special; then there's the black and tan colour—black all over with tan above the eyes, on the cheeks, inside ears, on the chest, on the legs and under the tail; the blenheim colour is a glossy chestnut with white patches; finally, there is tricolour, which is black and white with tan bits over the eyes, on the cheeks, inside ears and on the legs and under the tail. All the different colours were in this class. It was good that we can all get together to show off our humans. It proved the judges were only really interested in our humans, otherwise it would be common sense to split us up into our different colours.

We're very smart. All dogs are smart if they get the opportunity to train their humans properly. I sometimes think that humans think they're in charge. They could not be more wrong. Dogs rule the household. We're just clever in letting our humans think they know best. It's all part of training them.

Mistress was looking good. The class was so big that I thought it might take the pressure off her. The judge walked round looking at all the humans. Then I walked Mistress round the ring with all the others. This was going to take a long time. Eventually, it was my turn to get Mistress to lift me on the table properly. The judge looked at me all over, including my teeth. I think judges do that to distract Mistress and see how she reacts, but I know that the judges are actually checking out Mistress the whole time. I stood very still so that Mistress would behave well for this judge. Then I got to show her off by walking her round the ring by my side. She was walking well this time. Then, after we'd all done this, the judge came round again. I didn't think the judge rated my Mistress all that much because she didn't spend much time looking at her. Then the judge called a few of the humans with their dogs into the middle of the ring and sent the others away. And even although I didn't think the judge rated Mistress much, she was one of them. At least she'd get a fifth prize because there were now just five of us in the ring. The judge came round again, and we all got the chance to walk our humans up and down again. Then we all got to find out which of our Masters or Mistresses had won. Again the judge pretty much ignored Mistress. Then joy of joys, she picked my Mistress as first and handed her the red rosette. I could hardly believe it. She must have chosen Mistress from the start, which that why I thought she wasn't interested in her after that. I jumped up at Mistress to show her how pleased I was. I barked too, so that Reuben and Hugo could hear what had happened. They couldn't see from our cage. I was so delighted. I knew this was an important moment for my wonderful Mistress. I helped her to stand nicely by standing right in front of her, gazing up at her and wagging my tail while the judge wrote notes about how well-behaved she'd been.

All Mistress's friends were delighted for Mistress; Hugo, Reuben and I were really pleased too. We heard the Crufts word come up again as they talked. Now we knew she was on her way.

CHAPTER 30

Staying with Skye and Sarah

Reuben

How lucky am I? Mistress went out this morning, and when she came back, she put lots of my food and toys into a bag, picked up one of the dog blankets and put my lead on. I was so excited, this looked like some sort of a trip. Not a dog show trip, as there was no cage, trolley, green flask or folding chair, but this looked like some sort of trip. And then a very peculiar thing happened. Mistress didn't put collars and leads on Rufus or Hugo. Very odd behaviour. We never go anywhere without each other. Well not often. Sometimes Mistress takes us somewhere by ourselves and then we can share the tales when we get back. Like the time Hugo went out with Mistress to a very odd dog show, and she won a rosette without having to walk. The last trip I went on alone with Mistress was to see Sarah and Skye, the 'Mini Mistress' I told you about earlier.

Unless. Oh no. She couldn't be taking me back to my first Mistress could she? Don't get me wrong, I loved her dearly and it was fantastic to see her at dog shows. Especially if she had Teasle with her. I love Teasle. Just as much as I love Primrose. But I hadn't been on a trip with Mistress since she took me back from my last Mistress. How could I tell her I don't want to leave Rufus and Hugo? I grabbed my toy pheasant, one of my very favourites, and shook it at her. I gave it a really big, big shake. She just smiled and told me I was a good boy and that of course I could take pheasant with me. She was not getting it at all. I shook my pheasant harder. It was very difficult to get a whimper out when I was shaking pheasant so hard.

It was no use, it all happened so quickly. Hugo and Rufus were abandoned in the kitchen, just as confused as I was, and then she put me into the car. I did get to sit on the seat beside her, rather than in the back. This was another bad sign. This only happened when I was going to my first Mistress's house. I hadn't been there for a long time. Rufus and I were certain that I was staying with him forever. Mistress put the seatbelt on me. It's at times like this that I wish I could actually talk Human. Mistress was driving along, smiling, without a care in the world, and I was having a major panic attack. Which bit did she not understand? Just because my tail was wagging and I was fidgeting like mad, it did not mean that I was happy with the situation. It was very difficult to sit still when something as scary as this was happening. I was just going to have to accept the inevitable. As I tried to stay calm, I started to listen to some of the words she was saying and I heard "Skye" and "Sarah". I looked out of the window. Wait a minute; we came this way a while ago, just Mistress and me. This meant that after this car journey I would see Skye, and Sarah of course. Panic over. I wished I could have understood earlier and let Rufus know what was going to happen. He was worried the last time Mistress did this. Mistress took me on my own to see Skye, and Sarah of course. We went up to Skye's house in a place called Stirling that last time. She lives at the top of lots of stairs. Mistress had something to drink. So did I, and some biscuits, then Skye followed me all round her house to explore. Then Mistress and I went home. Well that would be OK, I didn't mind doing that again. I wasn't sure why the other dogs weren't with me. Maybe going to Skye's house was just a trip for Mistress and me.

I must have fallen asleep, but when I woke up the car stopped. And Skye and Sarah were there. They opened the door while Mistress let me out of my seat belt and put my lead on. I said a quick hello to Sarah, and then got Skye to lead me up all the way up the stairs to her house. This was great fun. I love Skye. Rufus says she's like a Mini Mistress. I love Sarah too, and always give her a special hug and as many licks as I can get away with. I'm good at licks. If I can get near someone's face, the chances are they'll get one of my special licks. Rufus says I have the longest tongue out of the three of us.

We went into Skye's house and guess what? My bed was already there, and some of my toys. I'd wondered where they'd got to. Skye took my lead off, and we checked the house. Mistress and Sarah didn't follow us. I realised they were in the kitchen talking about dinner and biscuits. Maybe I was staying for dinner this time. That would be good. Mistress seemed to have brought another bed for me. Sarah put the other bed into her bedroom. I wasn't sure what that meant, but I was far too excited to care. I sat down in front of Skye and gave her a paw. That was the signal I'd taught her to go and get a biscuit for me. She was very easy to train. After the third biscuit, Mistress spoilt it by putting the biscuits away. What she didn't realise was that I needed to keep on training Skye so that I could get her as well trained as Mistress. And that needed practice. And I couldn't practice without a constant supply of biscuits. Skye clearly understood this too, but Mistress was adamant. I think she is the Mistress to Skye too.

Sarah and Mistress put the bags with my dinner into a cupboard. I was allowed to have my toys in Sarah and Skye's living room. I was pleased and although confused, I thought I'd wait and see what would happen next. I wondered if I was meant to stay here forever. I love Skye. And Sarah. But I would really miss Rufus and Hugo. Still, as Rufus was always telling me, I have to trust Mistress and hope she knows what she's doing.

Then the next strange thing happened. Mistress gave me a big cuddle and asked Skye to look after me. It was such an odd thing to say. It was my job to look after Skye, not the other way round.

Humans are a bit simple at times. Then Mistress left and closed the door behind her. I looked at Sarah while Skye gave me a big cuddle. Sarah seemed to be trying to tell me it was a holiday, and I'd be staying with them. Well, I knew about holidays, but usually we'd stay in an unfamiliar house. How odd, I wondered where Mistress had gone. And I wondered why Rufus and Hugo weren't with me. I hoped Mistress would go straight back to them and explain where I was, and of course she would need looking after. I wondered how Skye and Sarah managed to cope without a dog to look after them all the time. Still with Mistress gone, maybe those biscuits can be put to good use.

I gave Skye my paw.

CHAPTER 31

Going to Crufts

Rufus

For some reason Hugo and I were left in the house while Reuben went out with Mistress in the car. This had happened a few days ago and when they came back, Reuben told us that he had been to visit Skye and her mum, Sarah. Maybe that was happening again. Why? The only other times Mistress went out with just Reuben was to take him for one of the outings we go on to practice taking Mistress out by ourselves from time to time; or back to his other Mistress. Reuben really loves his other Mistress, but he really likes being here with me. We all hope that he can stay here forever. Had Mistress given him away? He was doing fine here. And Reuben had got Mistress trained so well now. He wasn't nearly as desperate to protect her as he was when he first came to stay with us. Now he understood that the best way to handle Mistress was to get her to walk nicely beside him when a strange dog or human came close. He's done really well with her. Surely she hasn't taken him back to live with his other Mistress. What had Mistress done?

Hugo and I were a bit worried. When they left, Mistress took: a dog bed, dog food, biscuits and a few of Reuben's favourite toys. She didn't do that the last time. Hugo snuggled next to me in the basket in the kitchen. I tried to tell him not to worry, but it was hard because

I didn't really understand what was happening either. Eventually we fell asleep cuddled up together in our basket. We missed Reuben.

Hugo jumped up when he heard Mistress's car in the drive. Thank goodness, they were back. But it wasn't all right. Reuben wasn't with Mistress. She smelt of Sarah and Skye, so that was obviously where she'd been. She must have forgotten to bring Reuben back with her. That was very careless of her. Once she remembered, she would have to go back and get him. At least he was with Sarah and Skye. They love all of us so he'd be safe. Hugo couldn't believe Mistress had left Reuben behind. He searched the whole house in case he'd sneaked in and was hiding. Silly Hugo, the last thing Reuben would do was hide, he was far too nosey and bouncy.

Then Mistress went to the cupboard and got the dog show trolley out. A dog show without Reuben, surely not? She got out the black case that she keeps all of our dog show stuff in; then she put our brushes, water bottles and some other stuff into another bag. I tried to have a look to see what else was in it, but she shooed me away. What a cheek, I was only trying to understand what was going on. Then I knew we were going to a show. Mistress bathed and blow-dried Hugo and I. She put things in the car, and gave us our dinner. Then she had the cheek to go out. She was really pushing the boundaries, and keeping us guessing.

The next morning came and Reuben was still not home. Mistress seemed OK about this and kept telling us that Reuben was fine. She told us that he was with Sarah and Skye. Why? The only good thing about Reuben being with Skye and Sarah is that at least he could look after them.

We went for our usual walk, but it didn't feel right without Reuben. I normally tend to walk ahead, usually by myself unless there's a really good sniff that I want the boys to share. If we go on our walk over the big field and down to the dell, we run around together, but I usually do my own thing. Hugo sniffs around mostly with Reuben. Since he was a pup, he has always jumped over Reuben, and they push against each other as they run fast together. Hugo and Reuben regularly go back to check on Mistress during a walk, then run on ahead again. I always know exactly where Mistress is. She may not be able to see me, but I can sense where she is. Sometimes she calls for me, but as long as I know where she is, I don't bother going to her. I know by her voice if she's getting anxious about where I am, so then I'll usually make sure she can see me, before running off again. Of course she has a special tone in her voice when she needs to put our leads on. That's when we all go straight back to her in case she's in trouble. We know she feels much better if we're on our leads to protect her. There is the occasional exception—if we're chasing a rabbit or something. We know it can take a good bit of shouting to get us back. But sometimes we just have to do the dog thing.

That morning, Hugo wasn't sure what to do. Once we were off our leads, he was off, looking for Reuben. As if Mistress would leave him here in the dell. I barked at him and he came charging towards me. He started to jump around me and over me the way he does with Reuben. I just ignored him. He did it again. I growled at him. He looked confused. He pawed me on my back to encourage me to play. Sometimes Hugo can still be a real puppy, even though he's over two in human years. I stopped and let him sniff with me. Then he jumped over me again. That was quite enough, so I warned him with a big growl. Mistress saw what was happening and called for Hugo. She distracted him by throwing a ball. It seemed to work and I get on with the serious task of sniffing.

Once we were back at the house, we got our usual biscuits, but Mistress seemed to be very busy. After we had a sleep, she brushed us and got us into the car. Reuben had still not appeared. It seemed that we must be going to the show without Reuben. The only time this had ever happened was when he'd gone back to his other Mistress, and then I'd seen him at a show. I wondered if Mistress sent him back to his first Mistress, then visited Skye and Sarah. I was sure we'd find out eventually. I'd just have to trust Mistress, the way she trusts me.

We drove in the car for a while, and then Mistress stopped the car and got us out on our leads. We were at Rory, Mikey, and Leo's house, but we didn't have much time for exploring. Mistress put a cage in the back of their Mistress's car. It's a much bigger car than ours. We got put into the cage. We had our own blanket in the bottom of the cage. Surely Mistress wasn't sending us away too. Then Montie's Master arrived, and he put Montie into another cage on the back seat of the car we were in. Beside us in another cage was Mikey. It seemed his Mistress was leaving Rory and Leo behind. We all agreed that this was the strangest situation—with some of us dogs in the car, and others being left behind. This was going to be the strangest dog show we've ever been to. But I kept hearing the Crufts word again. It seemed that only some dogs are allowed to take their humans to Crufts. Which could only mean that Mistress behaved well enough with Hugo and me, but not well enough with Reuben. That was a shame. After what seemed a long time with all the humans chattering outside the car, Montie's Master, Mikey's Mistress and our Mistress get into the big car and we drove off.

Maybe this was going to be another big adventure. I wished Reuben was here to share it.

CHAPTER 32

A Very Long Drive

Hugo

The last couple of days have been very confusing. Reuben is nowhere to be found. I searched the house when Mistress got back yesterday, but he was definitely not in the house or garden. Rufus and I were sure Mistress would go and get him today. But no, instead she took just the two of us for a walk. It's been a long time since I went for a walk without Reuben. I tried to get Rufus to jump around with me the way Reuben does, but Rufus was having none of it. After a couple of attempts, Rufus warned me off, so I just had to settle for sniffing with him. He didn't even seem to like that for too long, so I got Mistress to entertain me by throwing a ball. At least when we got back to the house we got our usual biscuits.

After a while, we got Mistress to put us in the car by barking and carrying on. This tactic often works when we set out for a show. Rufus is particularly good at this. He doesn't often bark, but he does a good loud bark when he wants to go in the car, and of course, I happily take my lead from him. Mistress eventually understood and we got our way. She put us into the car while she finished off packing. That way we got to see exactly what she was packing into the car, instead of being left in the kitchen. Then off we went. Mistress stopped for a while at our friend's house and we got moved into another car.

We were clearly on the way to a dog show and Rufus and I were in a strange car with Mistress and our friends: Mikey and his Mistress; as well as Montie and his Master. We weren't even in our cage, it was one of Mikey's, but Mistress put one of our blankets into it to make us feel more at home. Rufus said it was best to settle down and see where we were going. We've been away with our friends before, and it was quite exciting. I usually speak to Mistress every so often on a long journey, so that she doesn't get too lonely, but I was very tired after looking for Reuben, so I slept most of the way. After a long time in the car, we all got out to sniff and pee, and it was then that I realised that it wasn't just us: Merlyn, a pretty Blenheim girl, and her Mistress; and Geordie, a Shar Pei, and his Mistress were also on the trip with us too. They were following us in another car. I kept hearing the word Crufts so I was sure that this was the show we were going to. Rufus agreed, but we both missed Reuben.

It had been a very long journey and it was dark by the time we got to a huge house. I think it was another hotel, well that's what the humans said. There seemed to be lots of other humans and their dogs staying at the hotel. There were all kinds of dogs, big and small. Mistress said, "Hello" to lots of people, and the nice ladies that helped us in the hotel patted us and told us how lovely we were. They were obviously not used to going to shows, otherwise they would have realised that it's not us who have to look nice—it's our Mistress.

We had a room that smelt quite good, and I was quite excited about sharing the room with Mikey and his Mistress. Mistress put our bed cover from home on the bed, so I knew it would be alright to snuggle with her.

I get a bit anxious when I'm away from home, so I didn't eat much dinner. Rufus was much braver; he seemed to take everything in his stride whatever happened. I just needed to be close to Mistress, and then I would be OK. We got taken out of the room and put back in the car. It was very dark outside now, but the car didn't move.

We fell asleep, and then Mistress came to get us again. I think she'd been somewhere where there had been human food. At least that was what she smelt like.

Mistress took Rufus and me out for a run, and then it was time for bed. I wanted to get as close to her as I could, so once she'd come to bed, I jumped up, put my paws on her shoulders and pressed my face against hers, giving her one of my "head hugs", which I know she loves. She moved me away. I did it again, but she seemed determined to get me to sleep in my usual place at the foot of the bed. She didn't seem to understand that I really needed to keep an eye on her. I knew Rufus was here, but he was already sleeping at the foot of the bed. He didn't seem to understand how much I missed Reuben. If Rufus was happy to sleep so far away from Mistress, then it was up to me to stay as close as I could to her. She had already lost Reuben. What if she got up during the night and got lost in this strange place? I really needed to be lying on top of her so that she would wake me if she moved, ensuring I could see what she was up to. I was very tired, but I was worried I might stay asleep if she wandered off.

I decided to do what I sometimes try at home when I need to keep a close eye on Mistress. I waited till she was asleep, and then I snuck up to snuggle in close. But every time I tried to snuggle on her head, she pushed me off. We eventually came to a compromise. I snuggled in under her arm. When she turned over, I climbed over her and snuggled in the other side. This seemed to work. Rufus said I shouldn't worry because surely she couldn't lose anything else.

CHAPTER 33

Rufus

Crufts It Is.

Crufts was the biggest dog show I'd ever been to. There were dogs and people everywhere. We got up early to get there from the hotel. Everyone was really excited. Hugo could hardly contain himself, he was even more bouncy than usual—and that was saying something. I tried to keep him calm, but it was impossible. We got out for a poo and a pee first thing, then got put into the car with the others. Mistress and her friends were very excited too, judging by all the non-stop chattering. Hugo and I were going to have to work very hard to get her ready for the show. We travelled to the dog show with Mikey, his Mistress, Montie and his Master again. It was great fun travelling with my friends. When we got out of the car, Hugo and I were put in a cage with Montie. I really like Montie. He's such a lovely, friendly tricolour, and he's managed to train his Master very well. His Master has won a lot of prizes; Montie is very pleased with him. Montie was hoping that if his Master behaved today he would win a prize. Montie has been to this big Crufts show before and he said it was very difficult to get prizes for our Masters and Mistresses here because they tend to get so nervous they muck it up. I knew what he meant. My Mistress would probably be too nervous to win anything.

Mistress and Montie's Master pushed the trolley with our cages on it over to the hall where the show was. It was a long walk for them, but maybe the walk would help to settle them down before we have to take them into the ring. There were dogs everywhere. I had never seen so many dogs. As we were on the way to the hall, we saw people waiting at bus stops with their dogs. Dogs on busses? I think I was on a bus once with Mistress, but there weren't any other dogs on the bus, just humans. We got to an enormous indoor hall that was full of tents with lots of doggy things in them.

When we got to the benches, there was enough space for our cage, Mikey's cage and Merlyn's cage all to be next to each other. This was good because it meant we could all keep an eye on our Mistresses. If they were together, they'd chat and that would help keep them calm. They'd have to be at their very best at this show. They took the brushes out, and we all got a bit of attention. They needed us to look our best so that we could have good control of them in the show ring. I could see Mistress checking that she had the rewards she's allowed to give us if she does well.

It was the kind of show where we couldn't see the ring. That was bad news. I warned Hugo that he wasn't to howl or bark while I was in the ring with Mistress. He sometimes does this, and I'm sure it puts her off if she can hear him. He was so excited that he hadn't stopped wagging his tail since he woke up this morning. I know he's young, but he needs to be a little calmer if Mistress is to do well.

Montie wasn't beside us any more; his Master had put his cage a couple of rows away from ours, so I wondered how his Master was doing. We waited patiently in our cages, with Mistress sitting next to us. Hugo was calmer now, and he even managed a nap. I let Mistress think I was sleeping, but if she made a move, I'd sit up. I could sense this show was very important to her, and I knew it was something that she hadn't done before. After a very long wait, and a share of Mistress's sandwich, it was Hugo's turn to take Mistress into the ring.

I wished him luck and told him to calm down so that he could get Mistress at her best, but he was very excited at being able to show her off at such a big show. It was a long wait until they came back. Mikey's Mistress got me out of my cage, as she sometimes does, and took me round to the ring. I could hardly believe the number of humans that were there. This show must be a lot more important than I had realised. I hardly had time to check how Hugo and Mistress had got on when I was swapped for Hugo. It was my turn to take Mistress in. Hugo said he had fun, but Mistress didn't get a prize. Hopefully she would do better with me.

The show ring was huge. The biggest I'd ever seen. It was covered with a kind of green carpet. I'd never seen anything like it. There were lots of dogs in my class showing their Masters and Mistresses, and we were all quite excited. I kept staring at Mistress to let her know just how proud I was of her for getting to a big show like this. Eventually it was Mistress's turn. She walked really well, and even managed to stand nicely while the judge looked at her. I felt very proud walking her round the big ring and showing her off to the huge audience and the judge. I had a very well behaved Mistress. The judge looked at all the humans very carefully and gave the ribbons out. Mistress wasn't a winner. I did feel sorry for her, she had worked so hard, and this was the biggest show of all. She seemed quite happy to have taken part, so I was glad she didn't seem too upset.

I got back to the cage and jumped in beside Hugo. We both thought Mistress deserved a prize. But at least we knew we'd be taking the very best Mistress home with us. We settled down, but after a while, she got both of us out again. And we were heading for the show ring again. This sometimes did happen. We thought Mistress must have asked the judge to give her another chance. Hugo would take her in, as he still needed the practice with her. He was much calmer now, so he'd be able to concentrate much better on getting Mistress to perform properly. I wondered which Mistress I'd have to take in. I did this sometimes when one of Mistress' friends needed some practice and didn't have a dog with her. I'm more than happy to help my human friends.

I'm very good at showing other dog's Mistresses. This time it was my doggy friend Merlyn's Mistress. I liked her; she's quite well behaved in the ring. I'd shown her before, so I knew that if she remembered her stuff, we'd be OK. It always seemed to happen when I was in the ring at the same time as Reuben or Hugo. I've shown lots of Mistresses. Maybe the other dogs think I'm good at it.

I watched Hugo go round with our Mistress. She walked up and down nicely with Hugo, who was clearly still a bit excited now that he was in the big ring. I knew how hard it was for him to stay calm, but he was doing OK. Mistress was doing very well; Hugo had her in check as she walked. Then it was time for me to show Merlyn's Mistress. She positioned me well on the table, and the judge checked she'd done it properly. Then I took Merlyn's Mistress round the ring. She did very well; she must have remembered all I taught her the last time I showed her. Then the judge walked around the ring and looked at all the humans again. We all stood around the inside of the big ring, hoping that our Masters and Mistresses would be the ones to catch the judges eye. He went over to his table and picked up the book in which he writes down all the marks for our humans.

Then it was time for the judge to choose his best humans. I glanced over at Hugo. He had our Mistress looking really good, and I hoped she would get a prize. But I knew I needed to do well for Merlyn. I was sure she would love her Mistress to get a prize too. I kept looking at Merlyn's Mistress. I tried to keep her attention so that she would stand nicely. The judge chose the humans for the red, blue, yellow and green prizes. I really hoped my Mistress would get the next prize. The judge stopped, and then looked at all the remaining Masters and Mistresses. He glanced at the dogs, but we knew he was looking closely at the humans. I was gazing at Merlyn's Mistress, all the time hoping that my Mistress would be the one to get the fifth prize.

But the judge walked past Hugo and towards me. Merlyn's Mistress won the fifth prize. I was upset it wasn't my Mistress because I knew she would be really disappointed, but maybe she would be happy that her friend had won a prize.

I had to line up with Merlyn's Mistress while the prizes were handed out. I could see Hugo and Mistress had left the ring. Everyone was hugging her. Although she was being very brave and smiling, all of her friends must have been consoling her that she didn't win.

When we left the ring, everyone told me how well I showed Merlyn's Mistress. I got lots of cuddles. It must have been because I did so well with Merlyn's Mistress. Hugo was still outside the ring, and he barked to let me know he was happy I did so well. We were both sorry Mistress didn't win, but from the way she was behaving, you would actually have thought that she did. I was glad that my Mistress was so happy that her friend had won a prize. Everyone else seemed very happy too. Then a curious thing happened: Merlyn's Mistress handed her prize to Mistress. That was really generous of her, and seemed to make Mistress so thrilled that she nearly cried, even although she hadn't really won it herself. Maybe if we got the chance to come to this huge show again, we'd get the chance to show Mistress off so well that she could win a prize of her own. I suppose that's what dog shows are—shows for dogs to show their humans. Crufts seemed to be the biggest and the best, so Hugo and I decided that we'd try to get Mistress there again.

Mistress is very lucky to have such good, kind friends. I could hardly wait to tell Reuben. I hoped I was going to see him again very soon.

Chapter 34

Home at Last

Rufus

We left the big show, very tired and happy. As well as Merlyn's Mistress winning a fifth prize, which she kindly gave to our Mistress, she won a fourth prize when Merlyn showed her. Montie's Master got a fourth prize, and Geordie, our friend the Shar Pei won a first prize with his Mistress. He was delighted, and had to take her back in the ring with the other Mistresses and their dogs. She didn't get another prize, but he was pleased with her performance. I sometimes get a bit scared of Geordie because he's so big and wrinkly. I'd love to meet him in a big park for a run around. I think if I got to know him a bit better, he might not be so scary.

It was a very long journey home and I was very happy when I smelt the familiar surrounds of the roads leading to our house. It was so late when we eventually got home that even the hens had gone to sleep. Hugo and I rushed into the house, but there was still no sign of Reuben. Mistress seemed to understand who we were looking for. Once she'd unpacked the show things, she cuddled us close on the couch and we understood the words: "Reuben", "Skye", "Sarah" and "tomorrow", amongst others. This was enough to reassure us that we would see Reuben very soon.

Mistress gave us our bedtime biscuits, and then we climbed the stairs to her room. Hugo and I cuddled down together at the foot of the bed. Hugo went to sleep immediately. As I dropped off, Mistress was reading a book and Hugo was dreaming. His paws were twitching, his tail was doing little wags and he was woofing very softly. The last thing I saw before I closed my eyes was my Mistresses lovely smile. She was murmuring softly to us as she often does as we go to sleep. I would have loved to creep up the bed and snuggle her close, but I was just too tired. And I didn't want to disturb Hugo when he was dreaming. I was happy to drift off with the sound of my beloved Mistress speaking softly to me. The only thing that would have made tonight better would have been if Reuben had been there. It felt a bit like when Reuben had to go back to his other Mistress from time to time. We thought those days were over, but nothing was certain. The thing about being a dog is that we trust our Mistresses completely. And we just follow our instincts to protect them, no matter what. I just wanted my brother back. I just wanted The Golden Boys back together to carry on with our adventures. I hoped that I'd see Reuben very soon. I could tell him all about our adventure, and I was looking forward to finding out exactly what he'd been up to.

Goodnight.

END NOTE

Rufus

I hope you've enjoyed hearing all about my friends and me. I have lots more to tell. And just so that you know, Reuben did come back. There is lots more to come in my next book, as long as I can get Mistress to write it so that you humans can read it. It's been hard work but I've trained Mistress to do all the writing. I have many stories to share, and this is just the beginning.

I will tell you about: what happened after Crufts, the deer down in Colinton Dell, the adventures in our new home, what happened to The One With The Beard, our unexpected next big move, coming face to face with a terrifying sheep, going to the beach with my friends, our Cavalier summer parties, unexpected friends coming to stay and so much more. And of course you'll be able to follow Mistress's success in the show ring.

See you next time.